How to Promote and Advertise

Published by :
Lotus Press Publishers & Distributors

How to Promote and Advertise

Michael E. Allen

Lotus PRESS
4735/22, Prakash Deep Building
Ansari Road, Darya Ganj,
New Delhi - 110002

Lotus Press : Publishers & Distributors
Unit No. 220, 2nd Floor, 4735/22, Prakash Deep Building,
Ansari Road, Darya Ganj, New Delhi- 110002
Ph.: 23280047, 98118-38000
• E-mail : lotuspress1984@gmail.com
www.lotuspress.co.in

How to Promote and Advertise

ISBN: 81-8382-015-8

Printed & Published by : **Lotus Press Publishers & Distributors,** New Delhi-02

PREFACE

Advertising and other types of promotional messages are used to sell products and services as well as to promote causes, market political candidates, and deal with societal problems. Everyone in our modern society is influenced by advertising and other forms of promotional activities. Today, the dynamic and fascinating field of advertising and promotion is undergoing dramatic and revolutionary changes. These changes are being driven by advances in technology and developments that have led to the rapid growth of communications through interactive media.

To advertise and promote products or services effectively in today's business world, it is essential that one should have a thorough understanding of the business environment and innovative ideas to use modern technologies for his/her job. This book provides succinct guidelines, useful tips and thought provoking ideas for effective advertising and promotion of one's business. It explains how to create, manage and produce cost-effective advertising, publicity, brochures, catalogues and public relations events. This practical guide will be an essential reading for anyone seriously considering the success of their business.

Editor

Advertising and other types of promotional messages are used to sell products and services as well as to promote causes, market political candidates, and deal with societal problems. To advertise and promote products or services effectively in today's business world, it is essential that one should have a thorough understanding of the business environment and innovative ideas to use modern technologies for his/her job.

This book provides succinct guidelines, useful tips and thought provoking ideas for effective advertising and promotion of one's business. It explains how to create, manage and produce cost-effective advertising, publicity, brochures, catalogues and public relations events. This practical guide will be an essential reading for anyone seriously considering the success of their business.

CONTENTS

1

CHOOSING THE MEDIUM FOR ADVERTISING

Media selection and placement is the full-time occupation of many people in large companies and advertising agencies.

1.1. BEST MEDIA FOR ADVERTISING

Choosing the best media for advertising depends on four factors:

1.1.2. Advertising Objective

What you want the advertising to accomplish and by *when*? Knowing what you want to accomplish is critical. It's not information to "just sorta have in your head." Your advertising objectives should be clear and written. Writing them down forces you to be specific.

These objectives should be part of your promotion plan. Most importantly, your advertising objectives should be something that *advertising* can accomplish. That may sound strange, but advertising can accomplish some things better than others.

Advertising can accomplish a shift in perception or create awareness, but–aside from specific adaptations of advertising–advertising alone can't create a sale. Many inexperienced advertisers think that *Advertising = Sales,* but that's an advertising myth.

1.1.3. Target Audience

Who and *where* are the people you want your message to reach? Take time to carefully define your audience. Certain media will have stronger appeal to some groups than others. Narrowing down your audience will help you make wise and cost-efficient media choices.

For example, the provider of a pet product might advertise in magazines or newsletters for pet owners. Additionally, this business owner may look for special ad placements, such as placing an ad in a special, one-time feature section on pet ownership published by the local newspaper.

1.1.4. Message and Frequency

What do you want to say and *how often* do you need to say it? The media you choose should carry your message effectively. Again, some simple logic will apply. If you have lots of information, don't choose a 30-second radio spot. If you need to show your product in action, don't choose any print medium.

If you need a message repeated with high frequency, for example "Sale ends in two days," you would not choose a weekly magazine where you would get one exposure, but you might choose radio where your ad could run periodically day and night.

1.1.5 Budget

It almost goes without saying, but your budget is probably the single most influential factor in your advertising plan. It might make all the sense in the world to place a TV ad or a full-colour advertisement in a prominent magazine–but you must be able to afford it! Your budget should be established and written out, too. The advertising budget is part of your marketing plan budget.

Buying just one TV spot is not an effective purchase since research shows that buyers need to be exposed to an ad several times before they take action on a message. But dollars alone should not be the deciding factor! If you could afford 16 spots on one radio station, 10 on another or one half-page newspaper ad, you would not automatically opt for the 16 impressions.

It's not that simple. You would also want to consider who listens or reads each medium, the timing of each medium, and the suitability of each choice for the message you want delivered, too.

1.2. MEDIA ADVERTISING

Advertising is paid, non-personal communication delivered through mass media. Media is part of the very definition of advertising. Advertising is a method of communication that is "paid" for and "non-personal." The message is delivered through mass media–as opposed to face-to-face, or voice-to-voice. So, the medium you choose for carrying your message is critical to the success of your advertising.

The following information will help you make good choices. But, always remembering thing is: You should consider each ad message or ad campaign separately. Just because a medium makes sense for one message does not mean it is the best medium for you all the time.

What you'll see is a list of things to consider when choosing your advertising medium. Remember, there is really no right or wrong medium. It depends on your message, your target audience, your objectives and your budget.

1.2.1. Advantages of Newspapers

1. Newspapers are still the number one media for local advertisers in terms of where advertising dollars are spent.
2. Daily newspapers reach a diverse (or broad) audience.
3. The audience is locally or regionally concentrated.
4. Consumers often look for ads in newspapers, so their mood may already be more receptive to your message.
5. Newspapers deliver timely messages because they have an established, regular publishing schedule such as daily, weekly or monthly. This allows you to tailor your message to current events, such as weekend entertainment or April tax time.
6. The immediacy of a daily newspaper's news will cause readers to pick it up within a predictable time frame (i.e. Tuesday's paper is usually read on Tuesday) so advertisers know when readers receive their messages.
7. Copy space is unlimited in newspapers. You can write long explanatory copy or a few bulleted lines. Of course, longer, bigger ads cost more.
8. Technology is improving newspapers' capabilities to create clear photos, better colours and to use new techniques such as scented inks.
9. Readers are actively involved in reading the paper. The fact that they must hold it and turn the pages produces a higher level of attention.

1.2.2. Disadvantages

1. Limits specific audience targeting. You may only want to reach bike owners, but you'll pay to reach the newspaper's entire audience. However, some papers offer "zone advertising" which allows you to run an ad that is seen only in part of the coverage area. For example, you could place an ad for your pizza delivery service in the "Northwest News" insert section delivered only with the newspapers in the northwest part of the city or newspaper coverage region.
2. Reproduction of photos has long been considered a disadvantage to using newspaper as an advertising medium, although technology has allowed great improvements. The problem is created because newspapers must use inexpensive paper to keep their costs down. After all, no one wants to pay $2.95 for a daily newspaper! However, inexpensive paper does not hold ink as well as higher grades of paper and that affects the clarity of pictures.
3. Many advertisers consider newspapers the best medium for local reach. This can create heavy competition inside the paper for local businesses. You may hear this referred to as "clutter."
4. Newspapers are not popular with all age groups. Their strength seems to lie with the aging Baby Boomers. Many newspapers are starting pages and sections designed for young adults, teens and kids, but the effectiveness of these efforts in terms of advertising draw is still not proven.
5. Newspapers are static and two-dimensional. Electronic newspapers may change this–in the future.

1.2.3. Advantages of Magazine

1. Great colour and photo reproduction are possible in magazines that are printed on slick or high-grade paper.
2. Selecting a targeted audience can be easy.
3. Magazines have quite a range of layout flexibility. Ads can contain colour or fragrance samples. They can have moving pieces, pop-ups, or carry microchips for sound. Photos can bleed off the page or fold out to larger sizes. This provides advertisers with many options for creating attention-grabbing ads.
4. Magazines have a long life span. People often save magazines to read at a more leisurely time. When a magazine is read over the weekend or on vacation, the ad is still there and the reader may be in a receptive, rather than rushed, mood.

1.2.4. Disadvantages

1. Because most magazines are printed on slick paper that makes for excellent reproduction, the costs are higher–to the consumer and to the advertiser.
2. The timing of reader exposure to your ad is less predictable. Most magazines carry more features than hard or breaking news, so reading can be delayed, and some ads could go out of date before they are seen.
3. Deadlines for placing advertising art are one month or more before publication. This means an advertiser must begin work on an ad long before it will be seen by the target audience. This often precludes small advertisers who leave advertising planning to the last minute from using this medium.

1.2.5. Internet Advertising

There are two primary ways to advertise on the internet:

1. Register your Web site with major search engines so internet visitors can find you.
2. Place an "ad banner" for your site on another Web site that has a lot of traffic (viewers). Ad banners allow viewers to link to your site when they click on the banner.

1.2.5.1. Advantages

1. Relatively cost-effective: The costs can also be independent of the size of the audience. For example, a Web presence will cost the same regardless of how many viewers your site has.
2. Advertisers can target specific types of viewers by positioning an ad banner on related Web sites: For example, if you're targeting people seeking information on a specific topic, you can purchase ad space on Web pages that are related to this category in the major search engines (Yahoo, Infoseek, Lycos, WONET - The Women's Online Network, etc.). So, an organic herb farmer selling through mail order might advertise through the "organic foods" or "gourmet cooking" category. The indexing structure of these sites allows you to target your audience by geographic location and related interest area.
3. Messages can be timely because editing the content is often easy and instantaneous.
4. Ads on the internet can be interactive. You can request viewer feedback, take orders or answer questions instantly.

5. Ad banners can run with as much frequency as you choose. The internet is constantly available!
6. Internet advertisers can potentially reach a global audience. Aside from language barriers, anyone at any location in the world can access information about your products or services.

1.2.5.2. Disadvantages

1. Internet advertising should not be approached in a vacuum. Instead, it should be one component of a comprehensive
2. Internet marketing strategy.
3. Although the popularity of the internet is rising remarkably, it is difficult to gage the impact of advertising on the internet.
4. The range of costs to advertise on the internet can vary greatly. It is best to compare a number of highly-frequented sites to determine the best way to spend your advertising dollars.

1.2.6. Advantages of Direct Mail

1. Allows you to target your message to a very specific audience. Pick one street of houses or all residents of a city. Target college freshmen or just college freshmen at one college who own a car. Mail to all of your customers or just to those who spend an average of $25 per visit to your store. The possibilities are as endless as your mailing lists accuracy allows.
2. This is a relatively expensive medium. However, if you are able to focus on only high-probability purchasers, cost effectiveness can be good.

3. Direct mail messages can be personalised to add reader appeal.
4. You can evaluate its effectiveness. If you compare the number of responses to the number of pieces mailed, you can calculate the response rate. If you include coded coupons or response cards you can keep track of exactly who responded and from where.
5. Mail readers are actively involved. People read their mail when they choose. So, for at least second or two, your message will have their undivided attention while they open and scan it.

1.2.7. Disadvantages

1. Many people don't like unsolicited offers and many are skeptical of their validity.
2. Increasingly, busy people don't even open what they view as "junk mail."
3. Using this method of advertising requires thorough maintenance of mail lists. Many advertisers do not like to bother with updating mail lists. With outdated lists, however, mail goes to undeliverable addresses and wastes your money. Another possible glitch: Mail may contain out of date messages, spell names wrong, or address a person who has died and these kinds of errors annoy, or worse yet offend, the recipient.
4. Some groups are concerned about the environmental impact of resources used for advertising mailings.
5. This is a relatively expensive medium.

1.2.8. Advantages of Radio

1. Radio messages are mobile: They can be heard at

work, on the beach, in the shower, in the dentist's chair or even while shopping in your store.

2. Radio is an intrusive medium. A listener does not have to be actively involved in getting your message to hear it.
3. Radio allows for target selection based on:
4. Geography - listeners will be in a concentrated area defined by the station's signal,
5. Time of day - the audience will change between morning drive, midday and overnight programming.
6. Format - different audiences can be reached by choosing different formats such as talk radio, alternative rock, blues rock, classical, easy listening, etc.
7. Depending on availability, it's often possible to get an ad on a station on short notice. This allows advertisers to react to sudden developments, such as a retailer selling fans reacting to a heat wave or a competitor's special offer.
8. Your message can run with as much frequency as you choose (or the station's format allows). For example, you could run an ad once a day for a year or twice an hour for a day.
9. Radio is mostly local in its appeal. You can tie your message into local events, weather, or locations to heighten the relevance of your message to the listener.
10. Your radio ad has a voice. It can be friendly, serious, sad, childish, macho, humorous–whatever suits your message. Above all, the voice can be conversational, a quality that makes it very easy to listen to and understand.

11. Radio time is relatively cost-efficient to purchase.
12. Radio ad production is fairly simple. Send a finished spot, a script or a fact sheet to the station and they will take it from there. Many will create the spot you want to run on their station for free.

1.2.9. Disadvantages

1. *Radio has no visuals*: Don't use it to talk about a product that a listener may not already understand. Some ads use "the theater of the mind" very effectively to create pictures in a listener's head. Be careful, though. This type of ad should be done well and may call for a professional writer–an extra expense that is well worth it in the long run.
2. *Some radio audiences may be "fragmented*: " For example, if there are four stations in the market that appeal to women 25-49 years old, then an advertiser may have to buy all four to effectively reach that group. This can be cost prohibitive.
3. *Air "clutter" is a problem*: Your ad may be first, second, sixth or tenth in a commercial break. This can detract from the attention level.
4. *There is no hard copy*: Your ad airs and then it's gone. If a listener missed an important piece of information, like a phone number, there is no way to know when it will be on again. (There are writing tips and placement plans you can use to minimize this problem.)
5. *Station-produced ads use station talent*: It's free and that's good, but you run the risk of the ad sounding very similar to other ads produced by the station and also to the DJ's regular on-air conversation. This sameness can detract from the listener's attention level.

1.2.10. Broadcast TV

Broadcast TV is "free TV" transmitted over the air and is most commonly associated with large TV networks such as ABC, NBC, CBS and Fox.

1.2.10.1. Advantages

1. TV offers your message sight, sound, motion, color and all the special effects you can afford. It is a powerful medium with sensual impact.
2. TV ads are intrusive in nature. The viewer does not have to be actively involved to receive your message.
3. TV allows for target selection based on:
4. Geography: Where the signal reaches.
5. Time of day: Different target audiences watch TV at different times.
6. Programme: Certain programmes or kinds of programming will appeal to certain groups. Observe the ads carried by a particular show. You can make some assumptions about who is watching, but for certainty about where and when to place your ad, seek the help of a media buyer or a TV rep.
7. Network: Some networks, like Nickelodeon or ESPN, have identifiable audiences that may match your target audience.
8. TV still has a certain prestige or glamour that can enhance your message. Some consider it "the big league" of advertising. You know, think of someone who saw her neighbourhood grocer in a TV spot–they'll often tell others (and the grocer) "I saw Jackie on TV!"

9. TV is costly, but because it may be targeted, it may be quite cost-effective.
10. TV ads can engage the viewer's emotions and empathy. You can see joy or hurt in someone's eyes, your can hear a voice tinged with the pain of a headache or the pride of a new parent, you can watch in amazement–or in disbelief–as a product is demonstrated.
11. Most TV is viewed at home. People feel safe at home and they aren't exposed to what others think. If they've been worried about aches and you have a message about how to cure them, you've got a listener and, hopefully, a customer.
12. Because of all the above, TV advertising is especially effective in helping to create an image for a product or company.

1.2.10.2. Disadvantages

1. To advertise on TV, you must produce a spot or pay to use one produced by someone else. Production fees on top of the cost of air time makes TV spots cost prohibitive to many advertisers.
2. TV seems complicated to small advertisers. If you think it is the right medium for your message, don't be put off by what you don't know–call a station or an ad or production agency for help.
3. Messages get "zipped" as viewers click to other channels and "zapped" as viewers mute them or turn them off.
4. Viewers that have grown up with TV and big-screen special effects are somewhat skeptical, if not downright cynical, about what they see. And they don't appreciate gimmicks.

5. Although TV can be targeted by geography, time of day, programmes and networks, it is still a broadcast medium with a broad, non-targeted reach. Cable is considered "narrowcast" and is a good, viable medium for reaching specific groups.
6. Audiences are more fragmented than ever as the number of channels increases, not to mention alternative uses for TV sets like video games, computer hook-ups and movie rentals. The days of any message reaching 40 percent or even 30 percent of the viewing audience on one network at one time are past.
7. Commercial breaks in programming are becoming more "cluttered." Your spot may be first, third or seventh in the lineup. The viewer's attention level can be affected.
8. Because TV is still considered by many to be "big league" advertising, small advertisers run the risk of looking amateurish next to a national advertiser with a slickly produced spot. There is some merit to looking like a friendly, small or local advertiser, but don't accept sloppy production in order to cut costs. No amount of savings is worth the damage you can do to the customer's perception of your business or product.
9. Buying TV time is fairly complicated. The help of an expert adds to your costs, but may cut your losses, too.

1.2.11. Advantages of Cable TV

1. You can buy time on programmes that have very specific audiences. For example, you might buy onto a show that is about caring for infants to reach young mothers, or you might buy onto a show

about sewing, wallpapering, landscaping, auto repair, local musicians, book reviews, etc. and reach a more clearly defined audience than if you bought time on a network show with bigger ratings and a higher price tag.

2. The cost is lower than broadcast TV because you are reaching a smaller audience.
3. Production costs may be more affordable.
4. You may find more innovative production people here. Often cable production teams hire young writers, producers and technicians who want experience and are eager to work with you. They are often right out of school and right on top of new trends and techniques.
5. Because cable only reaches into linked homes, you know who your message is reaching. These homes may be concentrated locally. Superstations are different: They reach huge cable audiences and charge accordingly.

1.2.12. Disadvantages

Almost all the advantages of advertising on cable TV have a flip side disadvantage.

1. Small reach.
2. May have less experienced production crews.
3. Reaching specific customers, but not reaching potential customers.
4. Cable TV as a whole is drawing huge numbers of viewers, but because of the increasing numbers of viewing choices, audiences can be very fragmented and viewers may stay with a programme for a shorter period of time.

1.2.13. Advantages of Transit Advertising

Transit advertising includes ads seen on buses, subway cars and entries, trains and taxis.

1. Exposure to one ad can be long if ad is inside a transit vehicle.
2. Frequency, the number of times a viewer is exposed to an ad, may be high if the viewer uses the same method of transportation repeatedly. For example, a person may ride the same subway to and from work 10 times a week.
3. Ads on the exterior of buses and cabs are seen by large and diverse audiences. You can also say that some of the audience is captive, too, if you consider the number of drivers stuck behind a bus or the number of walkers waiting for a stopped bus to move past.
4. The ad message can be timely because often the person riding mass transit is on the way to shop, eat or visit an entertainment outlet.
5. Ads can be geographically targeted because you know the people are all in a certain area at a certain time.
6. Ads can be somewhat lifestyle targeted, too. Some transportation travels through very distinctive neighbourhoods.
7. This method of advertising tends to be quite inexpensive in both absolute and relative terms.

1.2.14. Disadvantages

1. Your ad design is usually limited to the size of frames or holders you ad will be placed in.

2. People on mass transit are often not in a receptive mood or they may be so used to ads appearing in certain spaces that they don't even see them.
3. Transit ads are hard to target. Your ad reaches a lot of people, but many are not even potential customers.
4. You may not have mass transit in your advertising area. For example, many cities and towns don't have subways or bus service.
5. Subways, buses or other mass transit environments may not suit the product image.
6. The surroundings may detract from your message. A mud-splashed bus, a graffiti-sprayed subway car or a crumbling subway entrance wall may not be the showcase you had in mind!

1.2.15. Advantages of Billboard Advertising

1. Big, splashy messages attract attention. Using this medium you must be short and to the point!
2. Your ad has impact. Technology is allowing for more and more innovations like talking, moving, smoking, changing and twinkling billboards. Hot air balloons, blow-ups, flags, banners and other eye-catching devices are an option, too. You can even hire "rolling billboards" on the back of a truck that drives a route you choose to make sure your billboard is seen by the right audience numerous times.
3. Your ad reaches lots of people, many of whom see it repeatedly as they travel regular routes.

1.2.16. Disadvantages

1. It's hard to reach a specific audience. You might be

able to target a neighbourhood, but can't be more specific than that.

2. Your creativity is inhibited by space limitations.
3. It's hard to measure its effectiveness.
4. Your ad may become weathered or vandalised.
5. Costs can be quite reasonable for a billboard that you want to leave up for a sustained amount of time. However, innovative adaptations can become quite expensive.

2

THE ANALYSIS OF MARKET'S ENVIRONMENT

All of marketing is based on the idea that you must thoroughly know the environment in which your business operates in order to successfully promote and sell your product or service.

Ultimately, your idea must fulfil a need for your buyers and must do so in a way that's somehow superior to the competition, however you define it. If you want to be sure that your idea will do these two crucial things, you need to know as much as you can about the following:

2.1. YOUR COMPETITORS

The information age has increased the number of opportunities for new businesses and products and has tremendously increased the speed at which new products are developed and introduced into the marketplace. As a result, the information age has also increased the need for businesses to be thoroughly familiar with their competitors. In order to compete effectively, you need to know:

1. Who are your competitors?
2. What are your competitors' strengths and weaknesses?

3. What are your competitors planning to do next?
4. What are your competitors' spending trends?

2.1.2. Who Are Your Competitors

Your competitors are not always who you think they are. For example, if you are a manufacturer of popcorn products, your direct competitors are probably other brands of popcorn in the market. But what about tortilla chips, peanuts, snack mixes, or potato chips? And what about rice cakes, candy bars, cake/pie items, rolled candy, gum, or frozen confections? The target consumer may be making a choice among all these items for a "snack" purchase, including popcorn! Or the target buyer may be considering a drink purchase among alternatives for a "snack."

A company must narrow its choices and decide which industry, product or service categories, brands, geographic areas, channels of distribution, etc., to compete in. Without this knowledge and analysis, your marketing programmes will not be effective and efficient, particularly if you have a very limited budget.

2.1.2.1. .Competitor levels

It may help to think of your competitors as a series of levels, ranging from your most direct competitors to those who are more remote.

1. *First level*: the specific brands which are direct competitors to your product or service, in your geographic locality. In many cases, these competitors offer a product or service which is interchangeable with yours in the eyes of the consumer (although of course you hope you hold the advantage with better quality, more convenient distribution, and other special features). For

example, if you operate a local garden centre, you may compete against the other garden centres within a 10-mile radius.

2. *Second level*: competitors who offer similar products in a different business category or who are more geographically remote. Using the example of the garden centre, a discount chain that sells garden supplies and plants in season is also your competitor, as is a landscaping contractor who will provide and install the plants, and a mail-order house who sells garden tools and plants in seed or bulb form. None of these competitors provides exactly the same mix of products and services as you, but they may be picking off the most lucrative parts of your business.
3. *Third level*: competitors who compete for the "same-occasion" dollars. Inasmuch as gardening is a hobby, third-level competitors might be companies that provide other types of entertainment or hobby equipment; inasmuch as gardening is a type of home-improvement, competitors might be providers of other home-improvement supplies and services.

The point of this analysis is to consider carefully, from the buyer's point of view, all the alternatives that there are to purchasing from you. Knowing that, you can attempt to make sure that your business provides advantages over your competitors, beginning with those who are in the most directly similar to you. In fact, you can even borrow ideas from second- or third-level competitors in order to compete more effectively against your first-tier competitors.

2.1.3. Competitors' Strengths and Weaknesses

You should be very aware of your first-level

competitors— in many cases, you'll know them by name and may even belong to the same business associations they do. If you don't know much about their business operations now, make sure that you do soon! It's to your advantage to know as much as you reasonably can about the details of their businesses.

Study their ads, brochures, and promotional materials. Drive past their location. Talk to their customers and examine their pricing. What are they doing well (that you can copy) and what are they doing poorly (that you can capitalise on)?

Secondary data, as well as information from your sales force or other contacts among your suppliers and customers, can provide rich information about competitors' strengths and weaknesses. Basic information every company should know about their competitors includes:

1. Each competitor's market share, as compared to your own.
2. How target buyers perceive or judge your competitors' products and services.
3. Your competitors' financial strength, which affects their ability to spend money on advertising and promotions, among other things.
4. Each competitor's ability and speed of innovation for new products and services.

There may be a wealth of other facts that you need to know, depending on the type of business you have. For example, if you're in catalogue sales, you'll want to know how fast your competitors can fulfil a typical customer's order, what they charge for shipping and handling, etc.

Every competitor has definitive weaknesses and strengths that may be points of potential advantage for your company and products. In most cases, larger companies cannot make decisions or allocate resources, personnel, and materials as fast as a smaller company under changing market conditions. Smaller companies may have to be content with a limited, but profitable, objective of taking what they can from the market before larger competitors catch up later.

It is also important for smaller companies to decide when the cost of direct competition is both unwise and ineffective.

2.1.3.1. Cost of Direct Competition

Obviously, your most important objective as a small business is to survive and make money. Realistically speaking, there may be times when you'll decide, after careful analysis, that the competition in one area is simply too hot. Here are some situations that may indicate that the cost of direct competition is unwise and ineffective, from a sales and marketing perspective:

When you are faced with taking a loss on any marketing programme: Breakeven spending should also be avoided when done in response to competitive programmes.

When your direct competitor can outspend you both in money and quality of the offer: Larger competitors can almost always outspend you whenever you try to match one of their programmes. They can spend more money for longer periods and increase the depth and quality of their discounts and promotional programmes.

When your competitor's resources are significantly larger and more effective: It may make little difference if one of your direct competitors has eight sales people and you have six sales people covering the same geographic area and accounts. However, if your competitors can deliver programmes faster on a broader front and still not commit all their forces, you are significantly outgunned.

No battlefield general or business manager should risk a head-on confrontation.

When your competitor has more strategic and tactical advantages: Equal competitive resources may still be strategically and tactically more advantageous than your company's resources. For example, a competitor who spends the same amount in the same media but has higher recall/better-liked advertising has a strategic advantage. Or a competitor who has strong distributors in all your company's markets, while your company has a few weak distributors in the same markets, has a tactical advantage.

2.1.4. What Will Your Competitors Do Next

Once you know the identity of your most direct competitors and have a good idea as to your second- and third-tier competitors as well, you should give some thought to which actions they are likely to take in the next year or so. Estimates of competitors' future activity depend on your knowing and understanding their objectives, strength in the marketplace and resources. This important intelligence is key to your company's:

1. Annual forecast of sales, spending, and profits,
2. Promotion and advertising programmes,
3. Introduction, support, and success of new products and services,
4. Market, product, or service category, and sub-category trends,
5. Direction for future growth.

Gathering competitive intelligence can be the difference between realising your company's annual plan and losing business that may never be recouped. To be successful in identifying competitor's strategies and tactics, you must gather every bit of available data from sales forces, outside consultants, market surveys, and trade associations. For example, the data that you look at may include pricing, promotion and advertising spending, new product introductions, sales results, market share trends, packaging innovations, key account management, service levels, and other indicators of competitive activity in the marketplace.

The observance of competitive strategies and market tactics can be the basis for understanding a competitor's objectives. Is it simply profits and growth? Or could it also include "owning the market," driving other competitors out of the market, or being first in new markets and international markets?

Understanding each competitor's behaviour in terms of short- and long-term objectives, strategies, and tactics will be extremely important to survival and success, in business as on the battlefield. And many of the marketing programmes mimic battlefield moves. Dividing competitive forces among different markets, flanking attacks in weaker markets, direct frontal assaults with spending, new products and pricing across all market segments and product lines, and converting the enemy's best soldiers to your own company forces are all examples of tactics that may be open to you.

2.1.5. Competitive Spending Trends

Competitive spending trends may or may not be a significant influence on your company's marketing spending plans to support products and services. However, in a market where there are one or more large competitors, the amount of money your competitors are willing to spend will impact:

1. The success of your current products and services.

2. Your ability to obtain target buyers' attention and purchases.
3. Key accounts' attention and commitment to your programmes.
4. Your company's introduction of new products.

Every company can design and execute a competitive intelligence gathering programme that is cost-effective. It can range from simple secondary data information-gathering, sales force feedback, and trade publications/associations, to more sophisticated and expensive custom internal and external research.

Your company could design usage and attitude studies on target buyers, conduct focus groups, or do quantitative field studies. You could also examine industry subscription publications on specific industries and competitors or obtain volume-measurement services from ACNielsen, Informational Resources, Inc. (IRI), and other services such as custom-designed market simulation studies on competitive products.

2.2. YOUR TARGET BUYER

Do you know precisely who your customers are? You may know many of them by name, but do you really know what type of people or businesses they are? For example, if you sell to consumers, do you have demographic information that identifies your target buyer?

This type of information can help you in two very important ways. It can help you make changes to your product or service itself, to better match with what your customers are likely to want. It can also tell you how to reach your customers through advertising, promotions, etc.

For an obvious example, a company that sells athletic shoes may know that its typical customer is also a sports fan. Thus, if it can build shoes good enough to be worn by professional athletes, it will have a convincing story about quality to tell. It can also benefit by using well-known athletes as spokespersons in its advertising, and by placing advertisements in sports magazines where its customers are likely to see them.

How can you refine your understanding of your own customer base? We suggest that you look at the issue from two angles:

1. *Niche marketing*: identifying the heavy users of your product so you can direct your marketing efforts more precisely to those users.
2. *Segmenting the market*: dividing the existing market up into sections or segments that may become new niches for your business.

2.2.1. Niche Marketing

Most marketers know that "20 percent of buyers consume 80 percent of product volume." If you could identify that key 20 percent and find others like them, you could sell much more product with much less effort.

The "heavy users" of your product can be thought of as a market "niche" that you should attempt to dominate. Niche marketing today means targeting, communicating with, selling, and obtaining feedback on the heaviest users of your business's products or services. Picking the right segment of the market is important to achieving sufficiently large sales volume and profitability to survive and prosper as a company. Picking the right market segment means that it is:

1. Measurable in quantitative terms.
2. Substantial enough to generate planned sales volume.

3. Accessible to your company's distribution methods.
4. Sensitive to planned/affordable marketing spending events.

It is also important to examine other factors that could affect your company's success:

1. Strength of competitors to attract your niche buyers away from your products.
2. Similarity of competitive products in the buyers' minds.
3. Rate of new product introductions by competitors.
4. Ease of entry/protectability in the market for your niche.

Perhaps the driving force behind "niche" marketing, or "segmentation" is the need to satisfy and keep those consumers who really love your products or services. Consumers become increasingly more sophisticated and demanding. And product choices continue to expand with prosperity and world market competition.

Even large companies have embraced niche marketing, continuing to refine and target their product offerings to different buyer groups. As an example, Nike restaged a multi-billion dollar company that had plateaued by pursuing a segmentation strategy. Nike designed and marketed athletic shoes for each different sport, often further segmenting with specialised models within each sport.

It is also important to be able to identify and estimate the size of your target market, particularly if you're thinking about a new venture, so that you can tell if the customer base is large enough to support your business or new product idea. Remember that it's not enough that people like your business concept. There must be enough target buyers on a frequent-enough basis to sustain your company sales, spending, and profits from year to year.

2.2.2. Segment Your Market

If the universe of all potential buyers is your "market," then the market can be divided up into sections or "segments" based on any number of factors. For example, you might divide up your customers by age group and find that you sell most of your products to people aged 18 to 34. You might divide them up by family size and find that you sell most of your products to married couples with young children.

You might divide them up by economic status and find that you sell most products to people with an annual income of about $50,000 to $100,000. You might divide them up by geographic location and find that you sell most of your products to people living within two specific zip codes.

Many small businesses stop there, thinking they have enough information to be able to identify and communicate with their most likely customers. However, larger companies will attempt to push on further and find out even more information about their customers' lifestyles, values, life stage, etc.Let's define some terms:

Demographics: Refers to age, sex, income, education, race, martial status, size of household, geographic location, size of city, and profession.

Psychographics: Refers to personality and emotionally based behaviour linked to purchase choices; for example, whether customers are risk-takers or risk-avoiders, impulsive buyers, etc.

Lifestyle: Refers to the collective choice of hobbies, recreational pursuits, entertainment, vacations, and other non-work time pursuits

Belief and value systems: Includes religious, political, nationalistic, and cultural beliefs and values.

Life stage: Refers to chronological benchmarking of people's lives at different ages (e.g., pre-teens, teenagers, empty-nesters, etc.).

Customer and product data collection: Researchers gather data from users of similar products on:

1. Number and timing of brand purchases.
2. Reasons for purchases.
3. Consumers' attitudes about various product attributes.
4. Importance of the product to the lifestyle of consumer.
5. Category user information (demographics, psychographics, media habits, etc.).

Factor and cluster analysis: Researchers analyse the data collected in (1) to find correlations between product purchases and other factors, as a basis for identifying actionable consumer target "clusters." Clusters are defined as "niche markets," where there are identifiable numbers of buyers or users who share the same characteristics and who thus can be reached by adept advertising and promotion.

Cluster identification and importance ranking: Researchers then determine:

1. Whether clusters are large and viable enough to spend marketing funds on them.
2. Whether potential marketing niche clusters fit strategic company objectives; i.e., does marketing to this group fit your existing image and long-term goals.

Smaller companies can research secondary data sources and conduct individual interviews with key trade buyers and consumers or end users of their products and services (qualitative research). Often qualitative research can be accomplished for free or little expense. Smaller companies can also conduct informal factor and cluster analysis by:

1. Watching key competitors' marketing efforts and copying them.
2. Talking to key trade buyers about new product introductions.
3. Conducting needs analyses from qualitative research with individuals and groups.

In many cases, smaller companies have access to the same databases as large companies for estimating the sizes of market segment clusters and their importance. Some low-cost sources of external secondary data include:

1. Trade and association publications and experts.
2. Basic research publications.
3. External measurement services (large market research firms include ACNielsen, Burke, and Information Resources, Inc. (IRI))
4. government publications.

Smaller companies can segment markets by geography, distribution, price, packaging, sizes, product life, and other tangible factors in addition to demographics and lifestyle and psychographic clustering.

2.3. MARKETING ENVIRONMENT

Today's marketing environment is influenced by the global marketplace and the explosion of the information age to a degree unprecedented in history. To be fully prepared, a company must recognise and understand:

1. Cultural influences.
2. Governmental and political influences.
3 Demographic and lifestyle trends.

4. Local, national, and world economic trends.
5. The strengths of multi-national competitors.
6. The influence of technology on physical distribution.

Local, state, and federal trade organisations are often the best source of information on the trends that are likely to influence your business. The Government Printing Office (GPO) publishes many useful books to help you with research. If they're not in your local library, they can be obtained inexpensively from the GPO at your nearest Federal Building. Look in your white pages under the U.S. Gov't listings.

County Business Patterns: Put out annually by the Dept. of Commerce, each state bound separately, these provide figures on employment, payrolls, number of businesses and number of employees in each business class.

County and City Data Book: A book by the Census Bureau gives you information on housing, population, income, health, retail and wholesale trade.

2.3.1. Future of Market Growth

Once a market has been identified, what is the size of the actual market that you can compete in? The actual market segment that you can sell to may be a small fraction of the total market. Each total market must be examined in light of:

1. Size of the total market.
2. Size of the market that is interested in your products.
3. Size of the market that is available for distribution of your products.
4. Size of the market that already buys competitive products.

5. Size of the market that your company can serve.
6. Size of the market that your company can reach with advertising and distribution.

For example, the total potential market for water purification and filtering devices is 100 percent of the world's population, almost five billion people, since everyone needs to drink pure water. But the size of the market interested in water purification devices may be three billion people. The size of the market available for distribution may constitute two billion people. But the size of the market that currently buys such products may be under 700 million people.

Assume your company is planning to introduce new water purification devices only in the United States and only in the outdoor/camping industry for portable water purification devices. Then the total market you can serve for your company's products may be only one million potential users, or 0.02 percent of the total potential world market.

Depending upon your company's resources and size, you may be able to effectively reach only 50 percent of the one million American camping enthusiasts through distributors who are willing to take on your product line. Assuming you are able to afford a modest print magazine ad campaign in two or three national industry magazines, perhaps 50 percent of consumers may be aware of your products, or a net 250,000 potentially interested, aware consumers.

If only one in four interested, aware, available, and servable consumers end up buying your product, you have potential sales of 62,500 units/year. But if the repeat purchase rate is five years, you would need to generate an entirely new group of 62,500 qualified consumers each year, at least for the first five years. Perhaps you could increase the distribution base, increase advertising, or increase the served market to include other countries, or expand the product line by creating different sizes of portable water purification devices, or different units for varying severity of non-potable water conditions.

3

HOW TO MAKE A SUCCESSFUL MARKETING PLAN

The key component of a business plan is the marketing plan. Every business, small or large, will be more successful with a business plan. A good marketing plan summarizes the who, what, where, when, and how much questions of company marketing and sales activities for the planning year.

1. Who are our target buyers?
2. What sources of uniqueness or positioning in the market do we have?
3. Where will we implement our marketing spending plans?
4. When will marketing spending plans occur?
5. How much sales, spending, and profits will we achieve?

The financial projections contained in your business plan are based on the assumptions contained in your marketing plan. It is the marketing plan that details when expenditures will be made, what level of sales will be achieved, and how and when advertising and promotional expenditures will be made. Here are the major elements of a marketing plan:

3.1. SITUATION ANALYSIS

The primary purpose for the situation analysis section of a marketing plan is to describe what is happening in the markets in which the company competes, and the company's product and distribution trends.

Subsections should go from the "big picture" of macroenvironment influences on your business down through total market descriptions, the competition, target buyers/end users, and, finally, product trends and your company distribution channels description.

3.1.2. Macro-environment Situation

Macroenvironment situation describes only relevant information on macroenvironmental trends that might affect your business:

1. *Demographics*: For example, a home-building contractor should begin to pay closer attention to the needs of people over 65 (20 percent of the USA population will be over 65 by the year 2000) as baby boomers begin to edge closer to retirement. People are living longer and spending more on vacations, recreation, and entertainment.
2. *Economics/business conditions*: When interest rates go up because of inflation, the government is trying to slow business growth. Money is more expensive to borrow. People may be less apt to buy new homes or cars. International trade is affected by government tariffs and local labor costs and union organizations.
3. *Technological*: Innovation can create or wipe out industries and businesses in less than a year. The popularity and convenience of CD players all but eliminated the sale of record players and seriously depressed the manufacture and sale of vinyl records.

4. *Political and legal*: Health care and handicapped legislation affects all businesses, large or small. Increasing costs and mandatory provisions for buildings, walkways, elevators, etc., significantly affect the overhead for a small business. For example, a new restaurant with a basement must now have an elevator for handicapped employees, despite the unlikely circumstance of physically handicapped employees needing to go down to a basement storage area.
5. *Social and cultural*: There is a sweeping trend for Americans (and the world) to dress more casually, with function and comfort driving new clothing and shoe trends. People are cooking less and are more concerned about nutrition and fat in their diets. And today, American business people are less willing to sacrifice family life for business careers.

3.1.3. Market Situation

Market situation provides information on the size, growth, and trends of the overall market and any relevant segments of the total market or category.

For example, a small business could include local industry sales or volume for the last five years and estimated total market for this year and the following year, with company sales and share of the market. Rationale should be provided for estimating the trend of the market, including key industry developments, introduction of new technology or new products, increased marketing spending by key competitors, etc.

3.1.4. Competitive Situation

Competitive situation provides information about key competitors:

1. Description of key competitors and their market positioning.
2. Size of key competitors in units/dollars.
3. Market shares of key competitors.
4. Sales trends of key competitors.
5. Strengths and weaknesses of key competitors compared to your company's product or services.
6. Perceived marketing strategies of key competitors and their probable impact on your company.

3.1.5. Target Buyer or End User Situation

Tarsget buyer or end user situation provides actionable information on selling to target buyers and stimulating purchases or usage by the ultimate end users. Key questions answered in this subsection include:

1. Description of target buyers or end users in demographic, psychographic, and lifestyle terms.
2. Target buyer/end user wants, needs, attitudes, and perceptions of category products and services.
3. Where target buyers/end users are located and how to reach them.
4. Which segments of the total market or category are growing or declining and why.

3.1.6. Product Situation

Product Situation analysis company information on:

1. Sales.
2. Profit.
3. Product trends.
4. Cost-of-goods history (five years).

5. Marketing spending history (five years of advertising, promotion, PR spending).
6. Distribution trends and developments.
7. Description of the sales organization (e.g., company or brokers).

3.1.7. Distribution Situation

Distribution situation describes each distribution channel and its relative importance to the company in terms of:

1. Percent of company sales.
2. Company volume.
3. Cost to distribute products and services.
4. Growth potential.
5. Competitive status.

3.2. OPPORTUNITY AND ISSUE ANALYSIS

This section of the marketing plan analyzes the major external opportunities and threats to the company and the internal strengths and weaknesses of the company, along with a discussion of key issues facing the company.

1. External opportunities and threats to the company should be described with possible programs to capitalize on the opportunities, and possible solutions to potential threats to the company.
2. Internal strengths and weaknesses of the company should be described in a competitive context.
3. Key issues addresses decisions to be made by the company, based upon the analysis of these external opportunities and threats and internal company strengths and weaknesses, and helps to determine objectives, strategies, and tactics.

External opportunities may be seen in an analysis of the macroenvironment the company operates in. Other factors affecting your company may come from the market situation or the competitive situation that your company faces.

3.3. MARKETING GOALS AND OBJECTIVES

This section of the marketing plan outlines major company goals, marketing, and financial objectives. All objectives should be carefully quantified, where possible, especially in terms of an achievable time or date. Objectives should be reasonable and attainable. Major company goals could include both short- and long-term goals. For example:

1. Company definition (e.g., "to be a manufacturer of 100 percent all-natural snack food products")
2. Market definition (e.g., "to attain leadership in dollar market share and volume for the healthy, all-natural snacks segment of the salty snacks category")
3. Technology (e.g., "to become known in the industry as the leading developer of new vegetable protein products")

Financial objectives are generally described in quantitative terms for at least three years in the future:

1. Gross sales (increase).
2. Cost-of-goods (decrease).
3. Gross margin (increase).
4. Net income (increase).
5. Return on investment.
6. Return on income.

Businesses seeking outside funding and capital should provide a minimum of five years of projected income statements, although these are usually located in the financial section of the business plan rather than the marketing section. Marketing objectives are quantitative translations of the company's financial objectives, in marketing terms. For example:

1. Sales dollars.
2. Sales units.
3. Market share.
4. Distribution levels/channel.
5. Advertising awareness.
6. Key account distribution.

3.4. MARKETING STRATEGY

Every business owner should develop a written guideline that sets forth the business's marketing strategy. If a company has to take an action that is off-strategy, it may indicate a temporary emergency action prompted by competition or other factors beyond normal management control. Or it may indicate the need to change or revise the company's marketing strategy. A good marketing strategy provides specific goals and can include:

1. A description of the key target buyer/end user.
2. Competitive market segments the company will compete in.
3. Distribution channels.
4. The unique positioning of the company and its products versus the competition.
5. The reasons why it is unique or compelling to buyers.
6. Price strategy versus competition.
7. Marketing spending strategy with advertising and promotion.

8. Possible research and development.
9. Market research expenditure strategies.

An overall company marketing strategy should also:

1. Define the business.
2. Position the business as a leader, challenger, follower, or niche player in the category.
3. Define the brand or business personality or image that is desired in the minds of buyers and end users.
4. Define life cycle influences, if applicable.

Use the following checklist to help create your own marketing strategy.

1. Define what your company is.
2. Identify the products or services that your company provides.
3. Identify your target buyers/end users.
4. Establish the marketing category (e.g., fast food purveyor, high-end audio equipment sales, etc.).
5. Determine whether your company will be a market category leader, follower, challenger, or niche player.
6. Describe the unique characteristics of your products or services that distinguish them from the competition.
7. Define whether your pricing will be above, below, or at parity with your competitors and establish whether you will lead, follow, or ignore changes in competitors' pricing.
8. Identify the distribution channels through which your products/services will be made available to the target market/end users.

9. Describe how advertising and promotions will convey the unique characteristics of your products or services.
10. Describe any research and development activities or market research plans that are unique to your business.
11. Describe the image or personality of your company and its products or services.

3.4.1. Statement Strategy of Tests

If the statements in your strategy are measurable and actionable and work to differentiate your company and products apart from the competition, congratulations! If they are not measurable and actionable and do not differentiate your company from the competition, revise them until they are.

A good working marketing strategy should not be changed every year. It should not be revised until company objectives (financial, marketing, and overall company goals) have been achieved or the competitive situation has changed significantly, e.g., a new competitor comes into the category or significantly different or new products emerge from existing competitors.

3.5. SALES AND MARKETING PLANS

This section of the marketing plan outlines each marketing event or action planned to increase sales. The plan will generally cover a calendar year, broken down by month or by quarter. For example, it may contain a summary of quarterly promotion and advertising plans, with spending, timing, and share/shipment goals for each program.

Sales and marketing plans should be a logical outgrowth of short- and long-term company objectives and your marketing strategy. In the business plan, the sales and marketing plans provide an outline of each marketing event for the year, covering the following information:

1. Description of each event vehicle (e.g., media, promotion, trade, sales).
2. Timing of each event.
3. Event goals and objectives (e.g., volume, share gains).
4. Cost of each event.

4

HOW TO CREATE PROMOTION FOR MY BUSINESS

Public Relations (PR) activities are one way to promote the image or reputation of your business. PR is similar to promotion and advertising, but can be more indirect, since some or all of the publicity a company's products and services receive from public relations activities may not be controlled by the company. In order for your business to succeed, you generally need to promote your products or services to the same buyers that your competitors are targeting.

Even if your business is one-of-a-kind, you still need to tell target buyers that your business exists with some kind of advertising or promotional communication. If you're a big manufacturer of business-to-business goods, you may need to do much more personal sales promotion (to purchasing agents of your customer firms) than a consumer goods retailer, who would go to a promotion mix that emphasises paid advertising.

4.1. PLANNING OF PROMOTIONAL PROGRAMMES

Whatever you're selling, you'll need to communicate about it with your target buyers. Most businesses find that they need all three components of marketing communications (promotion, advertising, and public relations), in some combination. Determine who the target buyer is. Identification of exactly who the target buyer is, in demographic, lifestyle, and other descriptive terms, is necessary before the construction of practical promotion, advertising, and public relations (PR) programmes.

Determine what is meaningfully unique about your product. Many small businesses can describe what is meaningfully unique about their product or service. For other businesses, careful market research may be the only way to determine meaningful sources of uniqueness on product features and benefits. Meaningful differences are defined as those business or brand attributes that buyers or end users consider in making purchase decisions among different available choices. Customer perceptions control what is "meaningful."

Construct a business positioning strategy statement. It is important to be consistent in all promotion, advertising, and PR programmes, particularly with the scarce resources of most small businesses. A good business positioning strategy statement will address who the target buyer or end user is, what the competitive environment is, and what the meaningful differences in the products or services are when compared to the competition. The statement might also include reasons why these meaningful differences are valuable and perhaps some idea of a business "personality" that will be created and fostered in all marketing programmes.

Determine the best message to communicate your product positioning to target buyers. The key to communicating product uniqueness and positioning is constructing a memorable unique selling proposition (USP) about product features and benefits that are meaningful to your target buyer. This USP may be a memorable "slogan" or ad message that correlates with the needs and wants of your target buyer. The ad message is a result of a carefully constructed positioning statement.

Determine promotion and advertising options and costs in terms of available budget. There is never enough money to do everything desirable to build the business. Often a promotional budget reality check for a small business means a choice between a little promotion, advertising, or PR, but not all three at the same time

4.2. POSITIONING STRATEGY STATEMENT

Your business image is consistent to your target buyers/ end users and help to build an enduring, memorable (and hopefully unique) message to sell your business products. The following checklist can be used to help you organise the information needed to create a workable business positioning strategy.

4.2.1. Promoting Unique Selling Proposition (USP)

In this case, the message is targeted to all passing potential customers who want to indulge themselves inexpensively with a hot dog. There also may be a subliminal message for sinful or forbidden indulgence, too, since most hot dogs are high in fat and unsaturated fats. This unique selling proposition (USP) is self-targeting since only consumers who like hot dogs and feel that they deserve an inexpensive indulgence will believe this message is meaningful to them. Joe did not try to distinguish his hot dog features from those of other vendors (e.g., all-beef, skin-on, Kosher, etc.) since these features were not unique.

However, the benefits in his message are relatively unique: "inexpensive satisfaction plus indulgence." His informal, qualitative research revealed that his target market of busy office workers were constantly in conflict with themselves about wanting a juicy, delicious hot dog and trying to watch the fats and amount of meat in their diets. Therefore his USP and ad message were exactly on target for many customers.

4.3. MARKETING BUDGET

Promotion, advertising, and PR spending (i.e., "marketing support") ranges from less than 1 percent of net sales for industrial business-to-business operations to 10 percent or more, for companies marketing consumer packaged goods. Consumer packaged goods companies may spend 50 percent of net sales for introductory marketing programmes in the first year, subsequently lowering the percentage spent to a stable 8 percent to 10 percent within a few years. Retail stores that advertise and promote spend 4 percent to 6 percent of net sales for marketing support, on average.

Small businesses often estimate their sales revenue, cost-of-goods, overhead, and salaries, and estimated gross profit. Anything left is considered available funds for marketing support. A more rational approach is to estimate what your direct competitors spend in marketing support as a percentage of net sales and then try to at least match that amount.

If you are the new competitor in the marketplace, you will have to spend more aggressively to establish your market share objective. New business may come from expanding total product sales by attracting new users, as well as converting current users to your business from the competition. If you are an established business, your percentage of total expenditures for promotion, advertising, and PR should at least equal your market share, to maintain it. This rational approach assumes that all spending has equal effects on category buyers, which it may not.

4.3.1. Ideas of Promotion

Once a small business has determined both its business positioning strategy and the size of the promotional budget, specific promotional activities can be selected. Promotion programmes provide direct purchase incentives in contrast to most advertising, which provides reasons to buy your product instead of the competing brand.

Admittedly, some types of promotions can be expensive, complicated, difficult to execute, time-consuming, and difficult to administer legally. Many small businesses are local or regional, so some types of promotional activities will be too expensive or inappropriate for the type of goods and services offered.

The most important thing is to come up with a promotion that is unique and that sends the right message about your business. And it is critical to monitor the effectiveness of your promotions. If they don't generate results, they aren't worth the time or money you'll spend.

4.4. PROMOTIONAL ACTIVITIES

4.4.1. Games and Contests

Mass marketers frequently run games and contests on a nationwide scale. People look under bottle caps, collect game pieces, or submit entries in an effort to win prizes. Most small businesses probably don't need this type of promotion.

However, games and contests can be conducted on a smaller scale. For example, many restaurants ask customers to leave a business card in a bowl. Drawings are held periodically and winners are awarded a free meal or other prize. The restaurant owners, not incidentally, get valuable information in exchange for those prizes.

If your business is in an area with a lot of foot traffic, putting a game or contest in the window can draw additional customers into your store. It can be something as simple as the old jelly beans in the jar contest. If possible, use the contest to do double duty: in addition to getting the contestant's name and address, ask for information you need to better market your products or services. Be careful to analyse the results, though.

If none of the people drawn in the by the contest become customers, you're wasting time and money. Your promotions must be designed to get people to buy from you; the market research you can conduct is just a secondary benefit. Whatever games you devise, play fair with your customers.

Don't charge them to enter, and be sure to state how and when the winners will be selected, say that the offer is void outside of a certain area and after a certain date, and that any taxes are the responsibility of the winner. And be sure to check out the local laws with your attorney before you start any contest, game, or drawing.

4.4.2. Premiums and Gifts

Premiums and gifts, sometimes called "ad specialities," have been around a long time. The modern version of this free gift idea is aimed at name awareness: magnets, calendars, luggage tags, T-shirts, pens, pencils, or coffee mugs that carry your name, logo, and perhaps phone number or internet address. Anything that lasts and will be used by your prospective buyer can be effective.

For better or worse, there's already a wide variety of "standard" promotional items. Be aware of what's out there and be sure that your premium or gift is different and better. If at all possible, be sure there is a logical connection between the premium or gift and your business.

4.4.3. Coupons and Rebates

Many small businesses use coupons as part of their promotional programmes. The more common ones entitle the bearer to some benefit, such as a price reduction on a particular product or service. Others reward frequent customers for their loyalty.

Don't forget that only a small percentage of coupons are actually used. Newspaper coupon redemption rates in the grocery, drug, and mass merchandise industry average between 1 percent and 5 percent. Redemption rates for other coupon delivery methods (e.g., mail, magazine, newspaper four-color inserts) vary widely, but still amount to less than 10 percent for most products.

Coupons attached to the product itself are the ones that are most likely to be used, with redemption rates of 20 to 50 percent. However, these coupons tend to be redeemed by existing customers, so if your intent in distributing coupons is to get new customers, find another way to get them to your targeted audience. One good thing about coupons is that it's easy to monitor the results: you'll see every one that comes in.

A coupon should be good for at least 10 percent off the retail price of the product to attract buyers' attention and increase sales, with a 25 percent discount off retail considered more effective for mass market disposable consumer goods.

4.4.4. Product Demonstrations

Demonstrations are often more expensive per sampled target buyer when compared to advertising costs per target reached. However, demonstrations are many times more effective than single advertising ad exposures in any media. According to recent studies, because of sampling, 51 percent of shoppers tried products they normally would not have tried. And 79 percent of those sampled bought the product when they felt they needed it.

Demonstrations should be conducted at point-of-purchase whenever possible to maximise the opportunity for a buyer or end user to purchase immediately. It is estimated that over 85 percent of all grocery purchases are not planned in advance. Buyers purchase many items on impulse because of a product or service demonstration. Go to your local supermarket at noon on a Saturday and observe (and enjoy) the moveable feast the product demonstrators offer.

A promotion demonstration often takes the form of a free product sample or free trial service. Demonstration personnel also act as a mini-sales force in explaining product features and benefits and providing personal consumption and use testimony. A small business is well-served to arrange as many promotion demonstrations and sampling opportunities as affordable on a continuous basis to build business.

Also, demonstrations of products and services are the foundation for potentially free, word-of-mouth advertising, the most effective form of advertising known. While you will generally want to reach your target audience when you conduct seminars, you can also use them to build your business's community image.

You don't want to put on a blatant commercial — just an informative, generic talk will win friends and influence people. The residents of the center may not be your target audience, but if you favourably impress them, others in the community will hear about it.

4.5. IDEAS OF ADVERTISING

Advertising is impersonal, usually paid communication intended to inform, educate, persuade, and remind. Advertising is a sophisticated form of communication that must work with other marketing tools and business elements to be successful. Advertising must be interruptive — that is, it must make you stop thumbing through the newspaper or thinking about your day long enough to read or hear the ad.

Advertising must also be credible, unique, and memorable in order to work. And finally, assuming the actual advertising is built upon a solid positioning strategy, enough money must be spent to provide a media schedule for ad frequency, the most important element for ad memorability.

4.5.1. Word-of-mouth Advertising

Word-of-mouth advertising has existed as long as mankind has communicated and traded goods and services. Word-of-mouth advertising is considered the most effective form. Word-of-mouth has the desired qualities of strong credibility, high audience attention levels, and friendly audience reception. It features open-ended conversation with questions and answers about the product, psychological incentives to purchase, memorability, efficiency and frequency.

Word-of-mouth advertising passes product information to many other potential buyers (and may even include promotional trial demonstrations and free sampling), at little or no cost to the business. Whenever possible, a small business should build an advertising programme that results in word-of-mouth advertising! Satisfied customers are your best advertisements.

In some respects, typical media advertising acts only as a catalyst to achieve word-of-mouth advertising and increased sales. Successful advertising will achieve many times more ad mentions through word-of-mouth than the number of paid media presentations of the ads.

4.6. MEDIA OF ADVERTISING

There's an old adage that holds that at least 50 percent of all advertising is a waste of money. It's probably true — and if you can figure out which half of your ad budget is useless, you'll save a bundle. But until you achieve this wisdom (which has so far eluded most marketers), you'd be wise to continue advertising full tilt and not take a chance on eliminating something that just might work.

4.6.1. Low- and No-Cost Advertising

There are many things you can do in the way of advertising, promotion, and publicity that cost little or nothing. And when you become successful enough to be able to afford more sophisticated ad techniques, there are ways of measuring to some extent just how effective these methods are in terms of your business growth. As always, the chief concern is that the advertising do what it is intended to do cause more people to purchase more from your business.

4.6.2. Telephone Directories

Advertising in telephone directories is, for some businesses, critically important. But it's definitely not cheap. If you go with this kind of ad, check out the alternatives — Sprint, Ameritech, SBC, whatever baby

Bell you have in your area, as well as the cellular firms such as AT&T and Cingular and Verizon. Many areas receive directories published by more than one company. The cost of advertising varies, as does the market served. Try to pick the one that targets your potential customers the best at the lowest cost.

Even if you have to stretch to afford it, go for the bold-type listing if you can afford only a single line listing. If you can manage it, a display ad will probably pay big dividends if you keep it running year after year. Use strong black borders if possible and get the most size for the money without sacrificing placement. Don't be afraid to use lots of copy and use pictures and color (red is the usual alternative) if the budget can handle it.

Try to give your business a solid, dependable, reliable feel in your ad. If appropriate, say that you're insured or mention that you've been in business a long time. List every service you can think of as well as your hours and put some stress on your location so people can relate to it. The publisher's rep will give you guidance and examples of what you can do, but try to get a little edge of originality if at all possible.

The cost of your own 800 number may be less than you may think. Competition has made this a handy bargain way for buyers to reach you. The base charge is often around Rs. 1000 a month and 20 cents a minute with no special lines or equipment required. The calls can be forwarded to any line you choose.

4.6.3. Local Print Ads

Classified ads and small display ads in local newspapers or magazines are a good way to reach your buyers. Get media kits from all your local publications. Take a look at what they have to offer and at what price. The media kit will give you the demographic and geographic reach of the publication as well as rate information. Remember that the lowly classifieds are perused by a huge number of people, especially on weekends.

Big-time auto dealers and real estate agents fill these pages up for a reason. If you slip a classified ad into the right category and keep it running consistently, you'll probably get a response strong enough to at least pay the cost of the ad. The same rules apply to small display ads as to classifieds. Make it easy for your prospective buyers to learn what you have to offer. Use a border to set your ad apart if you can. Run the ad in the appropriate publication: do your homework, read those media kits. Make it very easy for your buyer to respond to your offer by giving a clear phone number, address and location details if space permits.

Another good way to reach customers is through your own newsletter. This can be a blend of advertising and informational text that refreshes your logo and identity and keeps you in touch with customers, without having to spend a mint on outside print advertising. Just be sure to keep your image consistent, wherever it is seen in print, and have it seen as frequently as you possibly can.

4.6.4. Signs and Displays

Signage is a key component of establishing and perpetuating your identity. Billboards, blimps, searchlights, and skywriting are exotic and expensive, so you'd be better served by concentrating on more down-to-earth signs. Start with your vehicles. Cars and trucks are great travelling billboards. You can readily find a magnetic sign supplier who can fashion a flexible rubberised sign to attach to your company truck or your personal car. When not in use for company business, simply remove the sign.

Employee uniforms are another form of sign. Your logo and identity must carry through all possible aspects of your business. T-shirts are great signs that even your customers can wear. Interior and exterior signs should be lighted to take advantage of every opportunity to be seen. Neon is becoming popular again, and creative things are being done in this medium.

Reader boards, those signs using individual letters so you can change the message at will, are very useful if well-positioned, lighted, and maintained. Zoning ordinances often limit the use of reader boards. These signs can be portable, on wheels, fixed to the ground in what is called "monument" style or, most often, high up on a pole. Changing the message often and avoiding misspellings will enhance their effect on your business.

4.6.4.1. Point-of-purchase displays

The importance of POP displays cannot be overemphasised. Impulse buying accounts for a huge amount of product sales. Service businesses can also use some POP techniques, especially when going to add-ons to a regular service such as "wax my car as long as you're going to keep it to change the oil" type of last minute decisions. But it's in the product realm that POP is king.

Often it's manufacturers who pay the cost of POP advertising. Providing a retailer with an attractive display is money well-spent by any manufacturer if it entices a retailer to feature the product and the consumer to purchase it on impulse.

4.6.5. Higher-Cost Advertising

If you get big enough to contemplate advertising in major newspapers or magazines or on radio or television, form your own in-house ad agency and save the usual 15 percent commission. This is as easy to do as printing up some letterhead with a name like XYZ Advertising Agency. Have a separate checking account if you're going to do a lot of this. This is standard procedure for medium-sized businesses who handle their own ad buys.

Of course, if you can afford it, you can hire a professional ad agency and learn the ropes before plunging in on your own. Sometimes the money they save you in good media buys may make up for their commission. The ad business is a very people-centered vocation so find someone with the kind of personality you'll be able to work with. They can also design and place infomercials if your product or service lends itself to this type of advertising. And don't forget the home shopping networks.

4.6.6. Electronic Marketing

Telemarketing comes in various guises. We all gripe about the computer-dialed boiler room selling operations that pester us at dinnertime, but there are other ways of using the phone as a sales tool. For a small business, it might be best to start calling people you've been referred to by current clients or networking contacts.

Look at telephone contact as a way of giving out information or keeping in touch, and avoid thinking of it as a way to close a sale. It gives you a chance for one-on-one contact but carries a risk of being intrusive. Calling on former customers to thank them for their business and inform them of new products or ideas you may have is a good way to keep in touch with a pre-qualified client base.

Cybermarketing is still a new frontier for most small businesses. Although it's considered poor "netiquette" to do any selling via e-mail, there are increasingly more opportunities via eye catching and invormative home pages to reach people and make it easy for them to reach you. This field is changing so rapidly that the best resource for evaluating your possible use of cybermarketing will be the many computer magazines on the market today as well as the vast array of information on the internet itself.

Creating and maintaining your own website is becoming easier and cheaper every day. And there are many excellent online catalogue and turnkey sales software products to help you establish your very own online store if you choose that type of distribution alternative for your business.

4.6.7. Direct Mail and Catalogues

Direct mail and catalogues are gaining enormous popularity. Firms like these are masters of database marketing. There are other hazards of direct mail, beyond getting the right list and creating a sharp, concise, attractive print piece. You have to maintain a flawless 800-number service with customer-centered operators who are your first line of contact with your customers. Then you must make sure your delivery services are prompt, your warehouse well-stocked, your order pickers mistake-free, and your merchandise return policies correct. On top of that, you must have truly superlative inventory management.

To start with, you may want to consider using a fulfillment house. These companies can take the calls, handle the customer credit process, and even ship the product if you wish. The fee is stiff but might just be worth it until you build a base.

4.6.8. Specialised Advertising Opportunities

Trade shows are essential to some types of wholesale and

manufacturing businesses. Display design, booth location and pre- as well as post-show mailings are carried to high degrees of sophistication (and expense). A small business person thinking of using this form of advertising would do well to contact the trade or professional association for his or her industry and also to pick up a copy of How to Participate Profitably in Trade Shows, by Robert Konikow, published by Dartnell.

Tie-ins with another business, co-op ad reimbursements from suppliers whose products you sell, and frequent buyer clubs are all becoming more prevalent in the current advertising environment. One of the emerging trends these days is for businesses to accept or even solicit the coupons of their competitors.

Public relations (PR) efforts, like advertising, can help to build business and product awareness among target buyers and end users, often at a fraction of the cost of advertising. Many small and large businesses consciously utilise PR as a way to obtain free advertising about their products and services. PR can be an effective way to generate valuable word-of-mouth advertising, sometimes due to the greater credibility and availability of information provided in editorial articles and interviews with your company personnel.

Free media publicity was largely responsible for the brief, frenetic ground swell for consumption of oat bran as an anti-cancer food. Melatonin, a naturally produced substance that aids sleep and may be an anti-aging product, is another PR craze, with newspaper, magazine, and electronic media discussing positive preliminary research results. Health food companies cash in on this free publicity, without spending funds for advertising, promotion, or public relations.

Snapple, the tea-based beverage, achieved sales in the hundreds of millions with zany PR programmes that generated millions of dollars in free publicity. After the Snapple brand was purchased by Quaker Oats, the zany PR stopped and sales declined. The Body Shop, an earth-friendly, pro-community/people cosmetics company with hundreds of millions of dollars in sales, works only with PR events to promote its business.

PR can leverage advertising and promotion programmes. PR events can leverage the effects of advertising and promotion programmes by tying all these marketing elements together. For example, a local on-site PR event for an automotive service company could include erecting a hospitality tent for company sales personnel to entertain key buyers at a local auto race. The local chain store buyers and car-owner end users could be exposed to ad messages on billboards, from announcers, and on race cars with the company logo. Buyers and end users could be given a free promotional sample to take home and try in their cars.

Public relations is an ongoing process and must be worked at every day on every level of your business from the way you deal with your employees to how quickly you shovel the snow from in front of your establishment. Make it a habit to constantly consider the image you are projecting. It's a good one to have.

5

METHODS TO PROMOTE AND ADVERTISE MY BUSINESS

Advertising is specifically part of the "outbound" marketing activities, or activities geared to communicate to the market, eg, advertising, promotions, public relations, etc. It is a major "phase" of overall product or service development and management. "Inbound" marketing activities are geared to communicate from the market, and include, eg, market research about the market.

Promotion keeps the product in the minds of the customer and helps stimulate demand for the product. Promotion involves ongoing advertising and publicity. The ongoing activities of advertising, sales and public relations are often considered aspects of promotions.

5.1. ADVERTISING AND PROMOTIONS

Advertising and promotions is bringing a service to the attention of potential and current customers. Advertising and promotions are best carried out by implementing an advertising and promotions plan. The goals of the plan should depend very much on the overall goals and strategies of the organisation, and the results of the marketing analysis, including the positioning statement.

The plan usually includes what target markets you want to reach, what features and benefits you want to convey to them, how you will convey it to them (this is often called your advertising campaign), who is responsible to carry the various activities in the plan and how much money is budgeted for this effort. Successful advertising depends very much on knowing the preferred methods and styles of communications of the target markets that you want to reach with your ads. A media plan and calendar can be very useful, which specifies what advertising methods are used and when.

5.1.2. Word About Writing Ads

It's almost useless to review lists of alternatives for advertising if you haven't developed well-written ads. Writing ads is a skill. There are important aspects to think about, including the wording, graphics, arrangement of wording and graphics, coloring, how your audience will interpret the ads, their placement, etc. Poorly done ads can hurt you worse than not having ads at all. Therefore, very carefully consider getting help to write your first ads.

5.1.3. Write in Your Ads

Almost entirely on the reading and listening habits of your current and potential customers. This is where some basic market research can help you a great deal. A lot can be learned by using a few basic methods. Before you write your ads, you should give careful thought to your unique selling position so you know what unique features and benefits to convey and to whom.

Your ads should clearly the benefits (of products and services) to customers, not the benefits to you — clearly state the ads in terms that the customer will value, for example, easy access, low cost, easy to use, reliability, etc. Your ads should answer the customer's question: "What's it it for me?" Your ad should also specify what they are to do next. What action should they take and how do they take it, for example, who do they call and how.

5.2. PROMOTIONAL ACTIVITIES

Articles that you write: Is there something in your industry or market about you have a strong impression? Consider writing an article for the local newspaper or a magazine. In your article, use the opportunity to describe what you're doing to address the issue through use of your business.

Editorials and letters to the editor: Often, programme providers are experts at their service and understanding a particular need in the community; newspapers often take strong interest in information about these needs, so staff should regularly offer articles (of about 200 to 900 words) for publication.

Press kits: This kit is handy when working with the media or training employees about working with the media. The kit usually includes information about your business, pictures, information about your products, commentary from happy customers, etc.

Press releases or news alerts: They alert the press to a major event or accomplishment and requesting, e.g., it get included in the newspaper; they explain who, what, where, why and when; some include pictures, quotes, etc. to make it easier for the reporter to develop an announcement or story.

Public service announcements (PSA)s: Many radio and some television stations will provide public service announcements for nonprofit efforts. Usually, these PSAs are free.

5.2.1. Other Promotional Activities

Annual reports: Disseminate these to key stakeholders; they're ripe with information if they include an overview of your year's activities, accomplishments, challenges and financial status. Collaboration or strategic restructuring - If you're organisation is undertaking these activities, celebrate it publicly.

Networking: Spread the word to peers, professional organisations and those with whom you interact outside the organisations, e.g., educators, consultants, suppliers, clients, etc.

Novelties: It seems more common to find ads placed on pens and pencils, coffee cups, T-shirts, etc. These can be powerful means of advertising if indeed current and potential customers see the novelties. This condition often implies additional costs to mail novelties, print T-shirts, etc.

Presentations: You're probably an expert at something. Find ways to give even short presentations, for example, at local seminars, Chamber of Commerce meetings, trade shows, conventions, seminars, etc. It's amasing that one can send out 500 brochures and be lucky to get 5 people who respond. Yet, you can give a presentation to 30 people and 15 of them will be very interested in staying in touch with you.

Relationships with key stakeholders: Identify at least one representative from each major stakeholder group and take them to lunch once a year. What seem as short, informal exchanges can cultivate powerful relationships of interest and concern.

Special events: These tend to attract attention, and can include, e.g., an open house, granting a special award, announcing a major programme or service or campaign, etc.

Special offers: We see these offers all the time. They include, for example, coupons, discounts, sweepstakes, sales, etc.

5.3. BENEFITS THROUGH ADVERTISING

Advertising, defined as "the action of attracting public attention to a product or business," is one of many marketing tools you can use to draw in more customers with greater frequency.

Also falling under the broad umbrella of marketing are public relations and promotional programmes, signage, premiums and incentives, newsletters, trade shows and word of mouth – in short, everything you do to help attain your company's overall goals. Ideally, your firm should invest in an on-going, consistent marketing programme using a combination of these tools for maximum impact.

5.3.1. Benefits through Advertising in Business

1. Remind customers and prospects about the benefits of your product or service.
2. Establish and maintain your distinct identity or "personality".
3. Enhance your reputation.
4. Encourage existing customers to buy more of what you sell.
5. Attract new customers and replace lost ones.
6. Slowly build sales to boost your bottom line.

5.3.2. Demerits of advertising

1. Create an instant avalanche of customers.
2. Cause an immediate sharp increase in sales.

3. Solve cash flow or profit problems.
4. Substitute for poor or indifferent customer service.
5. Peddle useless or unwanted products or services.

5.3.3. Virtues of Advertising

1. You have complete control. Unlike public relations efforts, you have final word in determining where, when and how often your message will appear, how it will look, and what it will say. You can target your audience more readily (working mothers, new home purchasers, small truck owners), and aim at very specific geographic areas.
2. You can be consistent, through advertising which presents your company's image and sales message over time to build awareness and trust. Similar to McDonald's golden arches, a distinctive identity can eventually become clearly associated with your company. People will recognise you quickly and easily—whether in ads, mailers, packaging or signage -- if you present yourself consistently through all the promotional vehicles at your disposal.

5.3.4. Advertising's Drawbacks

1. *It takes planning*: Advertising works best and costs least when planned and prepared in advance. For example, you'll pay less per ad in newspapers and magazines by agreeing to run several ads over time rather than deciding issue by issue. Likewise, you can achieve certain economies by preparing a number of ads at once.
2. *It takes time and persistence*: The effectiveness of your advertising is measured over the long run. That's

because people don't see every one of your ads. They only see some of them some of the time. You must repeatedly remind prospects and customers about the benefits of doing business with you. It's this constant repetition and the cumulative effect that win the day. It is also the long-term effort that triggers recognition and helps special offers or direct marketing really pay off.

5.4. STRUCTURE OF ADVERTISING

Think of the planning process as drawing a blueprint for your advertising campaign structure. First you design the framework, next you fill in the details, and finally you begin to build.

5.4.1. Design Framework

Start by defining your company's long-range goals. Then map out how marketing can help you attain them. Zero in next on possible advertising routes complementary to your marketing efforts, and be specific. Set measurable goals so you can evaluate the success of your advertising campaign. For example, do you want to increase overall sales by 20% this year? Boost sales to existing customers by 10% during each of the next three years? Appeal to younger or older buyers? Sell off old products to free resources for new ones?

How much can you afford to invest: Keep in mind that whatever amount you allocate is never enough. Even giants such as Proctor & Gamble and Pepsi always feel they could augment their advertising budgets. But given your income, expenses and sales projections, simple addition and subtraction can help you determine how much you can afford to invest. Some companies spend a full 10% of their gross income on advertising, others just 1%. Sorry, there is no fixed rule.

5.4.1.1. Fill in the Details

What are the features and benefits of your product or service?: In first determining the features, think of automobile brochures that list engine, body and performance specifications. Or food products that detail ingredients. Or accountants whose services include preparing tax returns and cash flow consulting.

Now the hard part: What are the benefits of those features to your customers? How does your product or service actually help them? For example, a powerful engine helps you accelerate quickly to get onto busy freeways. Certain food ingredients are cholesterol free or low in fat to aid in staying healthy.

Who is your audience?: Create a profile of your best customer. Be as specific as possible, for this answer will be the primary guidepost in creating your ads and choosing appropriate media.

Who is your competition?: It's important to identify who your competitors are, as well as their strengths and weaknesses. Knowing what your competition offers that you don't – and vice versa – helps you show prospects why your product or service is special, or why they should do business with you instead of someone else.

Knowing your competition will also help you find a niche in the marketplace and establish a particular positioning in your customers' minds. For example, is your product perceived as the most or least expensive? Are you regarded as a large or small company within your industry? Is your service seen as prestigious or utilitarian?

5.4.2. Arm Yourself with Information

What do you know about your industry, market and audience?: Many sources of information can help you keep in touch with industry, market and buying trends — without conducting expensive market research. Examples include U.S. Government materials from the Census Bureau and Department of Commerce. Public, business or university libraries are also a good option, as are industry associations, trade publications and professional organisations.

You can quickly and easily learn more about your customers by simply asking them about themselves, their buying preferences and media habits. Another alternative is to hire a professional market research firm to conduct your research.

5.4.3. Build Your Action Plan

Your next step is to select the advertising vehicles you will use to carry your message, and establish an advertising schedule. In most cases, knowing who your audience is will guide you towards the type of media that will deliver your sales message most effectively. Use as many of the tools as are appropriate and affordable.

Remember you can stretch your media budget by taking advantage of co-op advertising programmes offered by manufacturers to encourage you to advertise their products. Although programmes vary, generally the manufacturer will pay for a portion of media space and time costs, or mailer production charges, up to a fixed amount per year. The total amount contributed is usually based on the quantity of merchandise you purchase.

When developing your advertising schedule, be sure to take advantage of any special editorial or promotional coverage planned in the media you select. Newspapers, for example, often run special sections featuring real estate, investing, home and garden improvement and tax advice. Magazines also often focus on specific themes in each issue.

5.4.4. Using Other Promotional Avenues

Other options include imprinting your company name on pens, paper, clocks, calendars and other giveaway items for your customers. Put your message on billboards, inside buses and subways, on vehicle and building signs, on point-of-sale displays and shopping bags.

You can co-sponsor events with nonprofit organisations and advertise your participation. Attend or display at consumer or business trade shows. Create tie-in promotions with allied businesses. Send a newsletter. Conduct seminars. Undertake contests or sweepstakes. In addition, you can send advertising flyers along with billing statements. Use telemarketing to generate leads for salespeople. Develop sales kits with brochures, product samples or application ideas.

6

SALES FORECASTING

In an ideal world, the revenues would take care of all your expenses (and then some), and you wouldn't have to figure out how much more you'll have to pay to keep the business going. It might happen, but it's not likely to within the first few months of operation. Before we take a look at some ways to estimate revenues, a word of caution. Estimating your sales will be an inexact science.

Depending upon the type of business, there are a number of potential forecasting methods which should provide at least a ballpark estimate. For example, the National Restaurant Association and trade publication annual industry surveys provide a wealth of information about potential sales by type of restaurant food, price range, location, demographics, geographic marketing area, type of restaurant (e.g., fast food vs. family-style), and other statistics, along with average operational costs, gross margin, and earnings before taxes. Other trade associations, consultants, and the internet are excellent sources.

6.1. ESTIMATING SALES

6.1.1. Trade Publications

Your estimated sales figure is probably the most difficult

number that you will have to come up with in planning your new business. There are many variables and assumptions that come into play when estimating sales. Your location, marketing, competition, and business knowledge will have significant influences on your sales volume.

The sources for obtaining a reasonable estimate of future sales will vary by business type and individual. If you have significant experience in the type of business and are familiar with the local economic conditions, your prior knowledge may give you the best estimate. In this case, you will still want to back up your knowledge with outside verification. If you intend to get any outside financing for your business, you will have to justify your sales figures to your lender.

Most libraries have a wide range of information available for specific types of enterprises. The trade publications and trade associations are good sources of overall sales information for your specific industry. These publications will generally break out sales by geographic region and by business type. The publications may also provide key financial ratios that will be useful in your cash flow planning.

6.1.2. Product Vendors

Product vendors may be an excellent source of sales data. If your new business is one that will have high inventory levels, product or warehouse facilities may be a potential source of sales data.

For example, assume you plan to open a grocery store. You would purchase the majority of your product from a primary grocery distributor. Usually a distributor of any significant size will have access to other grocery stores' sales in your trade area. This could be your starting point for your sales potential.

You will have to make adjustments to the sales figure based, for example, on site selection, competition, and marketing. Be careful when dealing with product vendors to determine sales potential. Some may just tell you what you want to hear in order to get your business. Back up their forecasts with other sources.

6.1.3. Census Figures

The Bureau of the Census can provide you with a lot of information that can help you to estimate your projected sales revenue. For starters, Census demographic information can tell you the numbers and types of people who live in a specified geographic area, classified by age and sex. It can also tell you the number of households, the average household size, and the average, median, and per capita income levels in a given area.

The Census Bureau also tracks information on sales volume for various business types by geographic location. This information is available in most larger public libraries. It's usually a few years out of date, so if your new business is one that will be greatly affected by the time lag, you will want to make adjustments for it. Remember that any sales figure you come up with will still be just an educated guess. Along with the sales figure, Census publications will provide other financial details, such as cost of goods sold and payroll.

6.1.4. Cash Flow Peaks and Valleys

When small business owners plan their cash flows, they usually assume that sales will occur on a regular basis. For example, if they estimate that they will have Rs. 6,000,000 in sales revenue, they typically presume that they will do Rs. 500,000 per month in sales and plan accordingly. But the real world isn't always like that. Some businesses are seasonal, while others endure various ups and downs.

As a consequence, the business owner who has planned for Rs. 500,000 in sales revenue for a month in which he gets only Rs. 100,000 may experience a cash shortage because he hasn't planned properly. To combat this problem, here's what you need to know:

1. Cash flow forecasting: to begin with, all new businesses need to forecast their projected inflow and outflow of cash.
2. Looking at some cash flow what-ifs: what happens when your cash flow forecasts are off? You'll need to be able to respond to unexpected results.
3. Filling cash flow shortages: many small businesses turn to third-party financing when shortages occur.

6.2. FORECASTING SALES

Developing your sales forecast isn't as hard as most people think. Think of your sales forecast as an educated guess. Forecasting takes good working knowledge of your business, which is much more important than advanced degrees or complex mathematics. It is much more art than science.

Whether you have business training or not, don't think you aren't qualified to forecast. If you can run a business, then you can forecast its sales. Most people can guess their own business' sales better than any expert device, statistical analysis, or mathematical routine. Experience counts more than any other factor. Break your sales down into manageable parts, and then forecast the parts. Guess your sales by line of sales, month by month, then add up the sales lines and add up the months.

The illustration gives you an example of a simple sales forecast that includes simple price and cost forecasts which are used to calculate projected sales and direct cost of sales and estimate total dollar value for each category of sales. A complete business plan should normally include some detailed text discussion of your sales forecast, sales strategy, sales programmes, and related information.

6.2.1. Sales Strategy

Somewhere near the sales forecast you should describe your sales strategy. Sales strategies deal with how and when to close sales prospects, how to compensate sales people, how to optimise order processing and database management, how to manoeuvre price, delivery, and conditions.

Sales should close the deals that marketing opens. To help differentiate between marketing strategy and sales strategy, think of marketing as the broader effort of generating sales leads on a large scale, and sales as the efforts to bring those sales leads into the system as individual sales transactions. Marketing might affect image and awareness and propensity to buy, while sales involves getting the order.

Every business needs to forecast sales and then use the information to budget effectively. You can prepare a forecast based on your market research. Once you are in business, then existing sales can give a good indication of what you expect in the following period. You need to define your customers as accurately as you can - better still, name them. Look at the total size of the market; look at what your competitors are doing; read market research reports; look at what potential customers are buying; and undertake primary research. All of this should help you to set a forecast. For most businesses, the forecast is also the target, so put a sales graph on the wall and mark your target on it to give an instant picture of how sales are doing.

You need a sales forecast because your sales provide the income for the business. Without sales, you have no business. However a forecast will also enable you to set sales targets, budget effectively, and to prepare a cash flow forecast. Without an accurate forecast of sales, you will not be able to determine how much you can afford to spend.

A new business has no previous sales figures on which to base a forecast, so will need to carry out market research to prepare a credible forecast. Ideally, get promises of orders in advance of starting your business. Interview potential customers. Depending on your business and circumstances, you may be able to test the market with trial products, or start in your spare time before committing yourself completely.

Set a target for contacting potential customers. Some of these will turn into enquiries. And, in turn, some of these will turn into sales. As you gain experience, you will be able to estimate a conversion rate from original contacts, through to enquiries, and then to successful sales.

A sales forecast needs to be as accurate and reliable as you can manage. After all, you will be committing yourself to expenditure and loan repayments based on the forecast. If you underestimate, then you will not be able to cover your costs. If you overestimate, then you may not have enough working capital to cover your day-to-day cash requirements.

Remember, though, that there is a difference between forecasts and targets. Your forecast is your best prediction of what might actually happen. Use this to set your budgets and monitor carefully so that you do not overspend. In addition, you might set rather more stretching targets. If you achieve higher targets, then you will need to revisit the forecast and the budgets - but an ambitious target can be a real motivator to achieve higher levels of sales.

If sales are falling short of your forecast, then you will quickly run into problems. The most immediate effect will be lack of cash to pay your debts as they fall due. But your profitability will also quickly fall. So you need to act quickly to discover why sales are low and to remedy the problem.

1. Aim to raise the profile of your business through additional promotion - perhaps through advertising, but also through press coverage if you can manage it.
2. Revise your cash flow forecast and talk to the bank at an early stage if you think that the problem is temporary and that you will just need a short-term cash injection.
3. Take steps to cut out all unnecessary expenditure.
4. Keep a close eye on performance -if there is no improvement, then you may need to consider the future of your business.

If you need assistance to prepare a sales forecast - and a marketing plan - then there is help available. In the first instance, try one of the government-funded business support agencies or one of the local enterprise agencies. Depending on your specific needs, they may help directly or provide subsidised consultancy support. In addition, your bank manager or accountant may be able to recommend marketing support.

7

MANAGING MY ADVERTISING BUDGET

Once you accumulate date that enables you to determine the success rate of various sources of advertising you are able to apply this knowledge to the management of your advertising budget. Before you spend one additional dollar for advertising you should insure you have a detailed tracking system in place. At a minimum this system must be able to capture the following data:

1. Customer's name and phone number.
2. Method of inquiry – phone call or walk in.
3. Source of inquiry – newspaper, radio, television, direct mail, etc. If you advertise with multiple providers within these sources capture that data. For instance, if you advertise on two radio stations, have the customer identify the specific station.
4. Brief description as to the outcome of the inquiry.

The collection of this data must be complete and consistent. You must count every phone call and every customer that enters your lot. We referenced "contaminated" data. Make sure the scorekeeper or person tracking this data is diligent in determining the source of the customer inquiry. For instance if a customer claims to have responded to a television ad, you must determine what station.

The same goes for radio and print. Determine the real source. Don't let a salesperson enter "radio" for the majority of his or her calls just because that salesperson likes radio advertising. If this occurs, the result will be contaminated, meaningless data. Many dealers will appoint or designate a third party to count and track this data.

For instance, a receptionist or greeter may be charged with the task of tracking the above data for every customer inquiry. This person will either capture the data before transferring a call to a salesperson or have each salesperson register and "log" a lot up after the customer leaves the dealership.

7.1. BASICS OF ADVERTISING

The largest category in your advertising budget is likely to be your media costs – the dollars you spend for air time on radio or for ad space in newspapers, magazines, and more. Because of this, it makes sense to have a sound plan to manage that investment. You'll want to set goals. You'll want to describe strategies for achieving them. You'll have to organise the day-to-day tasks of carrying out the strategies.

The tool you'll need to do this is a media plan that begins with an overview and works its way down to the details. It will help you with every phase of your advertising. Here's how many businesses manage their media buying. The person in charge of the budget starts saying yes to the salespeople who call. Advertising appears here and there as a result. When the budget's gone, the person in charge starts saying no, and the ad campaign is over.

It's a method, but you wouldn't call it a media plan. And if that approach sounds familiar, you can bet you're passing up opportunities to maximise your return on investment.

Media planning is the process of choosing a course of action. Media planners develop yearly plans that list each media outlet – print or broadcast. Planning then gives way to buying, as each separate contract is negotiated, then finalised. A ring binder notebook is a good way to keep a media plan, because it's easy to update and easy to refer to. Or if you prefer to work on computer, simply think in terms of folders and files.

The media plan is a document in sections. A ring binder notebook is a good way to keep a media plan, because it's easy to update and easy to refer to. Or if you prefer to work on computer, simply think in terms of folders and files. The sections in your notebook will be:

Media outlets (newspapers, etc.): This section lists all of the media in which advertising will be placed.

Goals: This section describes the goals of the advertising, and explains why and how this plan meets these goals.

Audience: In this section, collect all the information you can about your target audience. You will want statistics by demographics or lifestyle; your professional association can help you find this information, as can trade journals or your banker. Pay attention to everything that helps you imagine an individual buyer who is typical of the whole.

Strategy: You will write a statement of strategy backed up by a rationale. The action steps you describe here will guide a year's activity.

Budget and calendar: Your media plan will outline what money is to be spent where, and when.

The document you've compiled in this notebook guides you in the execution of the plan throughout the year. Over time, these plans provide a history of your advertising. If you make alterations to the schedule in the course of the year, be sure to record those decisions in your notebook. Ring binders make it easy to update your plan as it evolves.

When you've finished this section, you will have an overview and the tools you need to create a media plan for your business. Let's start with basic vocabulary. The term you'll hear most often is CPM, or cost per thousand. CPM analysis is the method media buyers use to convert various rate and circulation options to relative terms. CPM represents the cost of reaching one thousand people via different types of media. To calculate CPM, you find the cost for an ad, then divide it by the total circulation the ad reaches (in thousands). By finding this information and calculating this cost for each of your options, you can give them a numerical ranking for comparison. CPM is a basic media concept.

Print advertising prices are based on the circulation of the publication in question. Publications will quote you a circulation figure based on paid subscribers. The audited circulation figures are verified by monitoring organisations. The publications will try to convince you that actual circulation is higher by including the free copies they distribute and the pass-along readership they claim. Sometimes these claims of "bonus" circulation are valid – for example, magazines distributed on airlines get at least eight readers per copy. Still, you should be wary of inflated circulation figures.

Audience is the equivalent of circulation when you're talking about broadcast media. Audience size varies throughout the day as people tune in and tune out. Therefore, the price for advertising at different times of day will vary, based on the audience size that the day-part delivers. Penetration is related to circulation. Penetration describes how much of the total market available you are reaching. If you are in a town with a demographic count of 200,000 households, and you buy an ad in a coupon book that states a circulation of 140,000, you're reaching 70 percent of the possible market – high penetration. If, instead, you bought an ad in the city magazine, which goes to only 17,000 subscribers (households), your penetration would be much less – 8.5 percent.

What degree of penetration is necessary for you depends on whether your strategy is to dominate the market or to reach a certain niche within that market. Reach and frequency are key media terms used more in broadcast than in print. Reach is the total number of people exposed to a message at least once in a set time period, usually four weeks. Frequency is the average number of times those people are exposed during that time period.

To make reach go up, you buy a wider market area. To make frequency go up, you buy more ads during the time period. Usually, when reach goes up, you have to compromise and let frequency go down. You could spend a lot of money trying to achieve a high reach and a high frequency. The creative part of media planning comes in balancing reach, frequency, and budget constraints to find the best combination in view of your marketing goals.

7.2. ADVERTISING BUDGET

You'll need to devote a percentage of projected gross sales to your annual advertising budget. A good rule of thumb is to devote 2 percent to 5 percent of anticipated gross sales to this need.

There are two primary methods of determining your advertising budget more specifically. First is the cost method, which theorizes that an advertiser can't afford to spend more than he or she has. For instance, using the cost method to determine the advertising budget, and devoting 5 percent of gross sales, a business projecting Rs. 15,000,000 in gross sales in a given year would have Rs. 750,000 for that year, or about Rs. 62,500 per month, to spend on advertising.

This may not seem like much money, and for some companies it won't be enough. These companies base their advertising budgets on the amount of money they need to attract the customer or sell the product. This is called the task method. A company using the task method typically determines how much money is needed based on past experience. Of course, as a start-up you won't have experience to go on. In this case, you'll have to base the figures on your business plan and market survey, which should estimate the costs you'll incur.

7.3. CALCULATE YOUR AD BUDGET

You're a very perceptive business owner. Budgeting 5 to 6 percent of total sales for advertising and another 5 to 6 percent for rent is the traditional wisdom. But as you suspected, this old formula is more tradition than wisdom, and it often results in too much or too little spent on advertising.

The purpose of advertising is to increase the exposure of your business beyond what is provided by your physical location. Yes, advertising and rent are both paid from the same bank account, and they both contribute to your overall visibility. True wisdom adjusts the ad budget by both the markup and the rent. Here's how to do it:

Calculate 10 percent and 12 percent of your projected annual gross sales and multiply each of these dollar amounts by the markup made on the average transaction. This will give you an adjusted budget range for total cost of exposure. In this first "adjustment" step, it's important to remember that we're talking about markup, not margin. Markup is gross profit expressed as a percentage of cost. Margin is gross profit expressed as a percentage of the selling price. Sell an item for Rs. 7500 that costs you Rs. 5,000, and your markup is 50 percent. Your margin, however, is only 33.3 percent.

This is because the same Rs. 2,500 gross profit represents 50 percent of your cost (markup) but only 33.3 percent of the selling price (margin). Most retail stores in America (carpet, jewellery and so on) operate on an average markup of approximately 100 percent, though some stores operate on as little as 50 percent markup and others add as much as 200 percent. More expensive items, such as cars, recreational vehicles, houses and the like, carry a markup of only 10 to 15 percent.

Second, we must convert 48 percent profit margin into markup, because markup is what we've got to have to make this formula work. To make the conversion from margin to markup, we simply divide gross profits by cost. Dividing Rs. 24,000,000 (gross profits) by Rs. 26,000,000 (hard cost) shows us that a 48 percent margin represents a markup of 92.3 percent. Bingo.

Now we multiply Rs. 5,000,000 by 92.3 percent to see that our adjusted low budget for total cost of exposure is Rs. 46,150,000. Likewise, we multiply Rs. 6,000,000 by 92.3 percent to get an adjusted high budget for total cost of exposure of Rs. 5,538,000. From each of these two budgets, we must now deduct our Rs. 180,000 rent. This leaves us with a correctly calculated ad budget ranging from Rs. 2,815,000 on the low side to a maximum of Rs. 3,738,000 on the high side.

Most organisations will tell you that 5 to 6 percent of gross sales is the correct amount to budget for advertising, but don't you believe it. It simply isn't possible to designate a percentage of gross sales for advertising without taking into consideration your average markup and your cost of occupancy. Yes, expensive rent for a high-visibility location is often the best advertising you can buy, since a business with a good sign in a high-visibility location needs to advertise significantly less than a similar business in an affordable location.

To prove this, just look at our example above and change the rent to Rs. 3,750,000 per year. The ad budget would now range from Rs. 5,865,000 to Rs. 1,788,000, representing only 1.7 to 3.5 percent of sales. This formula works because it reconciles your ad budget with your rent budget and considers the profitability of your average sales; it adjusts your advertising by both your markup and rent.

Each of the various ways in which to establish an advertising budget has its problems as well as its benefits. No method is perfect for all types of businesses, nor for that matter is any combination of methods. Here, concepts from several traditional methods of budgeting have been combined into three basic methods: percentage of sales or profits, unit of sales, and objective and task. You will need to use judgement and caution in choosing your method or methods.

7.3.1. Percentage of Sales or Profits

The most widely used method of establishing an advertising budget is to base it on a percentage of sales. Advertising is as much a business expense as, say, the cost of labour and, thus, should be related to the quantity of goods sold.

The percentage-of-sales method avoids some of the problems that result from using profits as a base. For instance, if profits in a period are low, it might not be the fault of sales or advertising. But if you stick with the same percentage figure, you will automatically reduce your advertising allotment. There's no way around it: two percent of Rs. 500,000 is less than two percent of Rs. 750,000. Such a cut in the advertising budget, if profits are down for other reasons, may very well lead to further losses in sales and profits. This, in turn, will lead to further reductions in advertising investment, and so on. In the short run, a small business owner might make small additions to profit by cutting advertising expenses, but such a policy could lead to a long term deterioration of the bottom line.

By using the percentage-of-sales method, you keep your advertising in a consistent relation to your sales volume, which is what your advertising should be primarily affecting. Gross margin, especially over the long run, should also show an increase if your advertising outlays are being properly applied. You can guide your choice of a percentage-of-sales figure by finding out what other businesses in your industry are doing. These percentages are fairly consistent within a given sector of business.

Knowing the advertising sales ratio for your industry will help you spend proportionately to your competitors. You must be careful however, not to base your entire budget on these reads. Every situation is slightly different and industry averages are only averages. Your particular situation may require you to advertise more or less than your competition. You may feel that at this point in your business life cycle, it is important to spend more than average on advertising the decision is ultimately yours. After all, growth requires investment.

No business owner should let any method bind him or her. It may be helpful for you to use the percentage-of-sales method because it is quick and easy. Not only is it a sound method for stable markets, but it may also keep your advertising budget from getting way out of proportion. Your budget can be determined as a percentage of past sales, of estimated future sales, or as a combination of the two:

Past Sales: Your base can be last year's sales or an average of a number of years in the immediate past. Consider, though, that changes in economic conditions may cause your figures to be too high or too low.

Estimated future sales: You can calculate your advertising budget as a percentage of your anticipated sales for next year. The most common pitfall of this method is an optimistic assumption that your business will continue to grow. You must always keep general business trends in mind, especially if there is the chance of a slump. Remember to assess the directions in both the industry and your own operation.

Past sales and estimated future sales: The middle ground between an often conservative appraisal based on last year's sales and an often overly optimistic assessment of next year's, is to combine both. This method is generally more realistic during periods of changing economic conditions. It allows you to analyse trends and results thoroughly as well as predict future sales a little more accurately.

7.3.2. Unit of Sales

In the unit-of-sale method, you set aside a fixed sum for each unit of product to be sold, based on your experience and trade knowledge of how much advertising it takes to sell each unit. For example, if it takes two cent's worth of advertising to sell a case of canned vegetables and you want to move 100,000 cases, you will have to spend Rs. 100,000 on advertising. If it costs X dollars to sell a refrigerator, you will have to budget 1,000 times X to sell one thousand refrigerators. Using this method, you are simply basing your budget on units of sale rather than dollar amounts of sale.

Some people consider this method just a variation of percentage-of-sales. However, since unit-of-sales is based on what experience tells rather than an overall percentage of your gross sales estimate, it is probably a more accurate estimate.

The unit-of-sales method is particularly useful in fields where the amount of product available is limited by outside factors, such as the weather's effect on crops. If that's the situation for your business, you must first estimate how many units or cases will be available to you. Then, you advertise only as much as experience tells you it takes to sell them. Thus, if you have a pretty good idea ahead of time how many units will be available, you should have minimal waste in your advertising costs.

This method is also suited for speciality goods, such as washing machines and automobiles; however, it's difficult to apply when you have many different kinds of products to advertise and must divide your advertising among these products. The unit-of-sales method is not very useful in sporadic or irregular markets or for style merchandise.

7.3.3. Objective and Task Approach

The most difficult (and least used) method for determining an advertising budget is the objective-and-task approach. Though it is more complex than other methods, this approach is the most accurate and therefore best method for determining your budget.

1. It relates the appropriation to the marketing task to be accomplished.
2. It relates the advertising appropriation under usual conditions and in the long run to the volume of

sales, so that profits and reserves will not be drained.

To establish your budget using this method, you need a coordinated marketing programme with specific objectives based on a thorough survey of your markets and their potential.

While the percentage-of-sales or profits method, determines how much you'll spend without much consideration, the task method establishes what you must do in order to meet your objectives. Only then do you calculate its cost.

You should set specific objectives: not just "Increase sales", but, for example, "Sell 25% more of product X or service Y by attracting the business of teenagers". Then, determine what media best reaches your target market and estimate how much it will cost to run the number and types of advertisements you think it'll take to get that sales increase. You repeat this process for each of your objectives. When you total these costs, you have your projected budget.

Of course, you may find that you can't afford to advertise as you'd like to. It's a good idea, therefore, to rank your objectives. As with the other methods, be prepared to change your plan to reflect reality and to fit the resources you have available.

7.4. ALLOCATION OF YOUR BUDGET

Once you have determined your advertising budget, you must decide how you will allocate your advertising dollars. First, you will have to decide if you'll do any institutional advertising or only promotional advertising. After you have set aside an amount on which to build your image (if that is your plan for the year), you can then allocate your promotional advertising in a number of ways. Among the most common breakdowns are:

Departmental Budgets: The most common method of allocating advertising dollars is "percent of sales". The departments or product categories with the greatest sales volume may receive the biggest share of the budget.

In a small business or when the merchandise range is limited, the same percentage can be used throughout. Otherwise, a good rule is to use the average industry figure for each product.

By breaking down the budget by departments or products, the goods that require more promotion to stimulate sales can get the required advertising dollars. Your budget can be further divided into individual merchandise lines.

Total Budget: Your total budget may be the result of integrated departmental or product budgets. If your business has set an upper limit for advertising expense percentage, then your departmental budgets, which are based on different percentages of sales in each area, might be pared down.

In smaller businesses, the total budget may be the only one established. It too, should be divided into merchandise classifications for scheduling.

Calendar Periods: Most executives of small businesses usually plan their advertising on a monthly or weekly basis. Your budget, even if it's for a longer planning period, should also be calculated for these shorter periods. It will give you better control.

The percentage-of-sales method is also useful here to determine how much money to allocate by time periods. The standard practice is to match sales with advertising dollars. Thus, if February accounts for 5% of your sales, you might give it 5% of your budget.

Sometimes you might want to adjust advertising allocations downward in some of your heavier sales months, so you can boost the budget of some of your poorer periods. But this should be done only if you have reason (as when you competition's sales trends differ markedly from yours) to believe that a change in your advertising timing could improve slow sales.

Media: The amount of advertising that you place in each advertising medium should be determined by past experience, industry practice, and ideas from media specialists. Normally, it is wise to use the same sort of media your competitors use. That is most likely where your potential customers look and listen.

Sales Areas: You can either spend your advertising dollars in areas where your customers already frequent, or you can use them to stimulate new sales areas. Whatever you choose, remember that it is usually more costly to develop new markets than it is to maintain the ones that are already established.

7.5. FLEXIBLE BUDGET

Any combination of these methods may be employed in the formation and allocation of your advertising budget. Based on your advertising needs, you may find that you need all or only one of these methods to meet your advertising objectives. Whatever the case, make sure that your budget is flexible. It must be easy to adjust when there are changes in the market.

The duration of your planning and budgeting period depends upon the nature of your business. If you can use short budgeting periods, you'll find that your advertising can be more flexible and that you can change tactics to meet immediate trends. To ensure advertising flexibility, you should have a contingency fund to deal with special circumstances—such as the introduction of a new product, specials available in local media, or unexpected competitive situations.

8

HOW TO IDENTIFY MY CUSTOMERS

Customers, every business has them, but why would you want to classify them. Are some customers worth more than others? Well, yes and no – some customers are more profitable than others are, while all customers could be equally profitable. Classifying customers helps you take the action right for them, targeting your marketing, and serving their different needs – while improving your profits.

Different customers require different actions to reach in marketing, to deliver your product to, or in how they implement your product. Your customers can be broken down into general groups reached with different triggers. Some customers are self-service, while others want you to come to them. Remember its "different strokes for different folks." Your ability to customise your marketing will determine how far you can reach into a targeted audience that will purchase your product.

Not only does each of your customers respond differently, but also they need to be marketed differently. Information gained from this understanding can improve the targeting of your customer lists, while you giving you a better response for your specific products. Group those customers with different qualifications; perhaps identify volume accounts verses infrequent buyers or premium product verses standard product purchasers. Those characteristics that make each group unique should be the strength that focuses your marketing to get the results you desire for your business.

We have talked a little already about the fact different customers have different needs, this is very important in classifying customers. These needs spanned product features, financing, shipping requirements, and any other aspect you could imagine in your business. Extending our thinking to look for cycles of individual purchases reveals other aspects of customer categorisation. If your product is consumed or wears out over a certain period, group together customers that may need a little call before their product runs out.

Another useful mechanism for categorisation is to find those customers that recommend your product, because they are a great channel to share new product enhancement or to tell about specials. These individuals are most likely to share the news or to communicate those things you make privy to them first. Categorising customers into groups by needs and identifying what is important to them allows you to serve them better while fulfilling their desires with your products.

8.1. SUPPLY CHAIN

As you get to know your customers, you may find that some customers are not the actual end users of your product. When classifying customers, understand not all customers may buy direct from you, but their needs have to be considered to maintain a viable product. Depending on what you are selling, you may find the actual end user is further down the line – this line we will loosely call a 'supply chain', which represents "how" your product gets to your customers.

With any analysis, we want to start with the beginning in order to gain the bigger picture of what is going on with our product before it reaches a customer. Start with the creation of the product (the beginning); do you manufacture the product or receive it completely from someone else.

Every time the product changes hands from one organisation to another, a little connection is made. You can represent this with simple boxes on paper, details on this will be provided later. This big picture approach gives you a better idea of the reach of your product; it could be anything from a screw in the back of a television, or the television itself.

If you manufacture a product, you probably sell it to a reseller or distributor who distributes it to your customer. If you sell directly to the customers themselves then that is fine too. In either case, there are three kinds of product providers, the reseller, the distributor, and the customer. The reseller receives your product to either incorporate it in their product, or turn it around to sell to their customers. Where a distributor sells to the reseller or sells at quantity to a particular customer. Finally, we all should know who the customer it is, they actually use your product to complete a specific task.

You can further classify customers into three types, even if you do not interact with the customers directly. The three customer types we are going to look are the manager, the end-users, and the integrator. Think of the manager as someone to obtain the product for end-users. The end-user ultimately uses the product for its intended purpose. Unless first an integrator received the product and incorporated it into something else the end-user uses. For example, an integrator receives software which is integrated into a computer system producing a the new product for an accounting department.

All of this will help you develop what should look something like a waterfall diagram with your organisation at the top. It is interesting but some products are created far from the intended end-user, the more uses your product has the more levels this diagram (your chain) may grow. Just remember, the end-user who finally uses your product, whether they know it or not, is where we are primarily concerned when increasing profits.

8.2. CUSTOMER

Classifying customers can improve profitability because optimisations along any of the connections in the supply chain can reduce costs without changing product sale price. If you can reduce your cost to manufacture and distribute your product then you can earn more per each transaction. In this section, we are going to talk about your customer, their customer, and the final customer – knowing that these levels could grow and expand depending on where your company is supply chain.

A clear definition of who purchases directly from you is the simplest and most direct part of classifying your customers. These individuals are the first level in your supply chain right under your organisation. These individuals are most likely buy from you directly for various reasons. Look further at those "reasons for buying" they determine how your customer connects to you. In most cases the customer will use the product themselves (end-user), while in others they turn the product over to the next level below them (reseller).

When your customers turn around your product it is good for you, even if the intended end-user could buy direct, sometimes resellers can reduce your distribution costs and increase product value. This important factor must be taken into consideration, especially if you want to maintain strong channel relations. Customers who buy directly from you are yours – those who purchase from the resellers are their own. Help your resellers and distributors to earn more, but do not steal their customers for the sake of direct sales it will only hurt you in the long run. In the case where you know who "their customers" are, you are in the fortunate position to help "your customer" with leads and growth opportunities.

Building the strength of your supply chain actually reduces your costs, even if "their customer" just turns around the product to a final customer, or eventually returns to you for services. The final customer, third down on your chart, actually uses your product (consumes) and usually does not turn the product around to anyone else. This is the target user that you do not always interact with directly.

At this level a lot of valuable information is available about replacements, renewals, and consumption. When you look at these individuals, also look at where this customer goes for help, perhaps they come back to you or they go to a vendor; either way optimising this part of the channel can improve product satisfaction and increased profits by identifying possible service opportunities.

A clear understanding of each "customer category" expectations and their usage of your product is so important to improve sales and distribution. You will want to make sure you get an accurate picture. Take the time to map this out, start with moment your product leaves your facility and move on from there. A simple diagram can say a lot about your business.

Your supply chain or distribution system as described here is very simple to map, yet so powerful. Start with a simple workflow diagram, move along to customer interaction points, and then finally clear up the picture with specifics. Creating a workflow is simple, just start with you and work your way out. For best results use a sheet of 11" by 17" paper –brainstorm first with customers and employees, then consolidate your notes, and finally enter your diagram into a computer using a simple flow chart programme. Don't go straight to a computer, brainstorm on a whiteboard or with paper, it's easier and takes less time.

Start with a box at the top of one page, this box is your company. Of the different types of customers described earlier, make a few blocks, representing them, just below your block. Use lines to connect each box representing the relationships between each, and then add simple labels to describe the boxes and corresponding relationships. Connectors represent delivery methods, transactions, or anything that would move a product from one box to another.

After you have drawn the relationships from your company to end user, it is now time to look at a valuable feature of this diagramming method, the "customer interaction points." A customer interaction point is anywhere along your chart where any customer talks to you. Concentrate on known ways your customer contacts you; this includes support calls, orders, presales support, and more.

Now that you have an overall workflow and it has been enhanced by customer interaction points, now you will want to start getting specific. This means adding in company names, points of contact, and customer category names. Your general boxes start taking life; a clear picture develops as the chart grows with information. Some organisation post phone numbers on these charts so they know whom to call during the customer service process – what you do with this chart after this point is unlimited.

Before you start turning this picture of your supply chain into a mosaic of information, remember why we created it in the first place. This picture represents everyone who uses or obtains your products in any form. Reconstruct this picture as often as necessary to develop groups that best represent your classifications of customers. Note at each level how you will market those customers, as well as their individual needs and expectations. From a marketing standpoint you must also consider where to gain the best results, incorporate this new information in your marketing tests or when considering lists.

If this exercise is difficult for your organisation, or if your chart seems too complex then you have a great opportunity to identify improvements for getting your product to market. Your entire supply chain should fit on one 11" by 17" sheet of paper in a very clear format that shows simple steps between levels – if it is any more complex than that, look for ways to simplify your distribution channels. By classifying your customers with a clear supply chain, you will see areas to reduce costs and increase revenues. Thos focus will increase profits for your organisation with very little effort on your part.

8.2.1. New Customers

You can grow an existing business by going after new customers who are in your area but who don't do business with you. There are lots of ways to do it. For example, you might change your pricing structure to reach up or down the economic ladder, or advertise in a different medium. But before you take the steps necessary to reach that new audience, a business plan can help you evaluate if the increase in business will justify the time and effort you'll expend.

How do businesses reach new customers? Some offer new products or services that appeal to people outside the existing customer base. The fast food chains did this when they began offering a wide variety of food outside the standard fare. A person who would never eat a fried hamburger might be willing to have a salad.

Fast food chains and others also try to attract new customers (and retain existing ones) by establishing drive-through service. Now, people who were unwilling to deal with parking are potential customers. The risk that the restaurants took was large. They had to redesign food preparation and service areas, install new equipment and fixtures, and completely alter the traffic flow through the parking lot. They didn't take the risk without carefully assessing whether the costs and required changes in operations would be worth it.

Are there people who never ate fast food before they could get it without leaving the driver's seat? Probably. It might not seem like a great basis for differentiating a group of people, but you can use a business plan to assess all the foibles of your potential new customers. You might be surprised at what you find.

8.3. BUYER IDENTIFICATION

Assuming that other factors in making the product available (distribution) and known to the buyer (advertising and promotion) are in effect, influences on the buyer may be catalogued by:

1. Culture.
2. Demographics.
3. Lifestyle.
4. Psychology of wants and needs.

If your target buyer is also the end user of your products and services, then demographic, lifestyle, and other target buyer identification and classification are appropriate. However, if intermediate buyers are involved prior to products reaching the end user, other influences may be important.

For example, consumer packaged goods such as food, health, and beauty aids and household products may be initially purchased in large amounts by a master distributor, who sells to local/regional distributors. These local distributors often sell to a wholesale buyer representing a chain of stores. Finally, individual store managers decide to buy and stock the product before the consumer ever has a chance to buy the product.

Other buyer influences may be at work under these circumstances:

1. *Profitability of the item*: The higher the margin and dollar profit per item vs. competitive category products, the more likely the trade will accept it, regardless of product quality.
2. *Discount deals available*: They can increase margin, volume, and velocity of the item. For example, 10 percent to 25 percent off invoice each quarter for all purchases during the period are typical discounts for grocery and drug retailers.
3. *Advertising and promotion support programmes*: Multimedia TV, radio, print and PR support, plus heavy consumer couponing, sweepstakes, and contests are typical consumer packaged goods programmes that may be run one to four times/ year.
4. *Other cash deals*: For example, new item "Slotting Fees" are the subject of controversy and frustration for many manufacturers supplying grocery, drug, and mass merchandiser retailers. Slotting fees are cash payments and/or free goods that are not refundable, even if the products are dropped after six months by the retailer. Slotting fees range from

a few hundred dollars to over $25,000 per item in some chains.

5. *Free goods available*: For example, one case per store is common for new grocery item distribution.
6. *Personal buyer/seller relationships*: There will always be personal relationships influencing buying decisions as long as there are people selling to people. That's why you hire good salespeople!
7. *Sales incentive programmes*: These programmes may spur salespeople on to greater productivity and sales of a particular item or offering.

For example, grocery buyers of consumer packaged goods may have strict profit margin guidelines (e.g., minimum 25 percent on discount retail price programmes), and minimum discount thresholds that they will accept (e.g., at least 10 percent off invoice). Buyers are also heavily influenced by brand advertising and promotion support programmes (e.g., coupons in local newspapers on the promoted brand). For new products, cash payments to the stores for each new item (e.g., $500 to over $25,000 per item) and free case goods on each new item for each store are common for larger chains.

The more exact the identification of your target buyer, the more efficient your marketing programmes will be in generating sales from regular or heavy users. We will divide target buyers into two groups:

8.3.1. End Users

If your customers are primarily the ultimate consumers or end users of your product or service, identification is generally done in terms of demographic and lifestyle factors. Demographics are tangible, measurable facts that distinguish one group of people from another. For example:

1. ethnic background
2. age
3. income
4. education
5. sex
6. location
7. occupation
8. number of people/family
9. children's ages

Lifestyle analysis is more concerned with the "intangibles:"

1. cultural background
2. religious beliefs
3. political beliefs
4. value systems
5. recreation and hobbies
6. music preferences
7. literature preferences
8. food preferences/menu planning
9. restaurant preferences
10. entertainment preferences
11. travel preferences
12. social interaction patterns
13. media habits

For example, heavy coffee, liquor, and tobacco users are not easily identified with demographic information. They may be found in any age group or socio-economic category. However, lifestyle analysis shows high correlation with certain characteristics, including media habits, recreational pursuits, social interaction patterns, music, and other attributes. If you can identify these, you can make your promotions or advertising more appealing to these target buyers.

In some product categories, such as alcoholic beverages, there are several skewed segments representing different age groups, demographic characteristics, and lifestyle patterns:

1. An 18-to-30 age group, primarily male heavy beer drinkers, with subsegments differentiated by choices of country and western music, rock music, contemporary/jazz, and sports interests.
2. A 39-to-55 age group including both males and females, with an urban skew and subsegments with wine and hard liquor, differentiated by classical, jazz, new age, and soft rock music, with interests in reading, movies, heavy video rentals, more expensive vacations, and both younger and older children.

8.3.2. Channel Buyers

If you sell to other businesses, who turn around and resell your products and services, your buyers are predominantly channel buyers. Examples of channel buyers from the grocery and drug industry are:

1. Total country master distributors.
2. Local/regional distributors.
3. Chain store wholesaler buyers.
4. Individual retail store buyers.

Influences on channel buyers may include non-target identification attributes such as the item's margin and profitability, discounts, free goods, cash fees, and personal relationships.

Channel buyers may be subdivided into:

1. Business-to-business markets.
2. Government.
3. Consumer markets.

Business-to-business and government buyers. Business-to-business and government buyers are subject to many different influences than buyers of consumer goods:

1. Fewer buyers.
2. Larger business transactions.
3. Regional concentration of buyers.
4. Defined sales and broker relationships.
5. Dependent upon end-user buying patterns and demand.
6. An inelastic market, meaning that the demand for goods and services is not significantly affected by a significant change in price

Business buyers take many factors into account when contemplating buying decisions:

1. Macroeconomic trends, nationally and internationally.
2. Long-term material supply trends and inventory needs.
3. Delivery rates, timing, and reliability.
4. Plant capacities.
5. Suppliers' financial resources.

Consumer-goods buyers. Consumer-goods buyers are subject to different influences when compared with business-to-business and government buyers:

1. There may be many buyers at multiple levels in the same company.
2. Small to large transactions.

3. National, regional, and local buyer concentration.
4. Direct company sales to buyers, or broker relationships.
5. Directly dependent upon end-user buying patterns.
6. End users influenced by company advertising and promotion spending.
7. An elastic market, meaning that the demand for goods and services is easily affected by slight changes in price.

Channel buying decision influences: Channel buyers may or may not directly purchase company products and services. There are many different roles in the buying process for a large supplier's customers:

1. Purchasing department personnel.
2. Buying committees.
3. Department advisors.
4. Consultants.
5. Management.
6. Head buyers and assistants.
7. Store managers.
8. Department managers.

It is not uncommon for a new item survey to be conducted throughout a majority of a chain's stores, with purchase intent/store/quantity indicated by store managers. The new item may be reviewed by all those listed above to ensure margins, store policies, technology, distribution systems, warehousing, shelf life, retail pricing, promotion programmes, and profit goals and standards are being met by the company supplier.

Ideally, you should always research and test your idea against the realities of the marketplace. Many business owners have tested their ideas by working as employees in their industry for a number of years and have seen firsthand what works and what doesn't. But even well-seasoned industry experts can benefit from analysing the market environment in a way that will help to evaluate the potential of an idea.

9

HOW TO PROMOTE MY BUSINESS IN LOW COST

Business promotion is to running a successful business as practicing scales is to playing the piano well; it may not be a thrilling activity in itself, but you just have to do it. You should spend at least an hour a day on business promotion or planning how to promote your business. You promote your business by getting the word out.

9.1. BUSINESS PROMOTION

The first axiom of business promotion is that you have to do this consciously. You can't rely on other people to do it for you, no matter how great your product or service is.

The second axiom of business promotion is that like every other aspect of your business, it's a budgeted activity. But business promotion doesn't have to be expensive. Here are ten inexpensive ways to promote your business; all most of these will cost you is some time.

9.1.2. Use of Paper and Electronic Document

For instance, business stationery is an ideal business promotion tool. Is your business name, logo, contact information (including URL if you have one), and slogan on your envelopes as well as on your letterhead? Or are your envelopes only printed with your business name and return address? What a waste! Your phone and fax numbers, your URL, and even a memorable slogan should be there, too. It's not just an envelope, it's a business promotion tool! You're sending it out anyway, so why not make it work for you?

The same goes for outgoing faxes, bill payments, receipts; whatever paper you send out should carry your full company message. And don't forget to make sure that your email has a complete signature that provides all your business information and a promotional tagline.

Electronic documents, such as email, are also easy to update with your latest business promotion information, whether it be a special price on your product or service, or letting people know that your company has won an award. If you need information about using signature files with particular mail programmes, visit About Email Guide Heinz Tschabitscher's Signature links.

Articles and press releases are also excellent business promotion tools that you can use to promote your business inexpensively. Read on to learn what types of articles and press releases you should write and tips on where to send them to promote your business effectively.

9.1.3. Articles and Press Releases

Well-written articles can provide free advertising and build positive word-of-mouth. If you're a realtor, for instance, you could write a piece on preparing your home to be shown. If you're a Web site designer, you might write a piece about assessing Web site usability. The more specific your topic, the better. Write a short biographical note, or "blurb" about you and your business to go with the article.

As the goal is to promote your business, ideally you'd like it to appear in a publication that your target audience will be reading. Realistically, you may have to send it to a publication that accepts unsolicited work from unknown authors.

Newspapers are also excellent places to place your business promotion article, as they too have a much shorter lead-time than magazines, and are always looking for material. Try contacting the Business editor of your local paper and pitching your article. If this approach fails, you might be able to get your piece into the paper by sending it in as a letter to the Editorial section.

9.1.4. Sending Out Press Releases

The caveat to using press releases as a business promotion tool is that your press release has to actually contain information that is newsworthy, and be engaging enough to get people's interest. Has your business recently expanded? Do you have a new product? Have you been involved in some promotional activity such as sponsoring a charity event? Have you or your company recently won an award? All of these are examples of "news" that you can capitalise on to get some free promotion for your business.

While many business people send press releases to newspapers as a matter of course, don't forget about the Internet. Web sites like mine, for example, that specialise in providing business-related information, are interested in you and your accomplishments.

9.1.5. Forums, Buddy Marketing and Freebies

Posting messages in forums is a great way to make your business known to people you would otherwise be unable to contact. You can't blatantly advertise your business on most forums, but you can show others that you're a knowledgeable, personable individual and promote your business through your signature file.

Getting people interested in your business and perhaps attracting new customers works best if you choose forums that are business-related or directly related to your business's product or service.

The other caveat with choosing forums to post in is to check their level of activity; posting in a forum that doesn't have much traffic or regular activity isn't going to do much to promote your business.

9.1.6. Give Out Freebies

We're all familiar with hearing or reading advertisements that promise that the first 50 people to visit a particular store will receive a free product. It could be anything from a red rose through an ice-cream cone! We're all familiar with this kind of spot promotion because it works. People love to receive things that are free.

Besides using freebies as business promotions, you can also use them regularly as customer "rewards". Still looking for more low-cost business promotion ideas? Talk show guest and giving seminars as ways to effectively promote your business.

9.1.7. Talk Show

Your local radio station or cable TV station may have programmes that are looking for guests - a great low-cost way to promote your business! Business-related programmes are ideal. Find out who the host is, and approach him or her as willing to share your expertise on a particular topic.

Call in programmes are popular; you may be able to appear as a guest expert. If you're a mechanic, you might offer to take call-in questions on car maintenance; if you operate a health store, you might market yourself as an expert in herbal remedies. Have your proposal clearly worked out before you contact the programme host, and make sure the parameters of your appearance, such as details about plugs, are clear beforehand.

9.1.8. Seminar or Presentation

You have expertise that other people are interested in. Why not share that expertise and promote your business at the same time? For example, a local carpet company advertises a free seminar on installation techniques for a type of laminate flooring.

Participants not only learn how to install this type of flooring themselves, but are offered special discount prices if they wish to purchase laminate flooring. Another local retailer who sells goods made of stained glass offers courses on working with stained glass on-site.

If there's no direct tie-in to your product or service, you can still give a presentation on a related topic. Nursery people or horticulturalists, for instance, often give demonstrations on topics such as tree-pruning, or slide shows of famous gardens they've visited.

If it's not feasible to present the seminar at your site, because you're a home-based business or just don't have the facilities you would need, arrange to give the seminar elsewhere. Many government-sponsored organisations, such as Business Service Centres and Econonmic Development Centres, and non-profit programmes are always looking for experienced business people who are willing to give presentations. You may also be able to arrange to present your topic through the Continuing Education branch of your local college or university.

Start small and start building a name by making a presentation to one of your local groups such as your Home-Based Business Association or Business Women's network.

That's eight low-cost ways you can promote your business so far. But there are two more business promotion opportunities that you may not have considered yet; using your car and your non-business related activities.

9.1.9. Use Vehicle

Mobile business promotion isn't just for white delivery vans. One in every four vehicles has the name and phone number of a business decorating one of the windows or doors. Think of all the people who see your vehicle when you're driving around - especially if you live in a place where people often get stuck in traffic.

9.1.10. Lesiure Activities

You may not be part of a band yourself, but everyone does something for "fun". Whether your chosen leisure activity is working on a Spitfire Restoration project, rock-climbing, or shopping, there are all kinds of ways to promote your business while you do what you love to do.

Where's the harm in shopping or rock-climbing wearing a T-shirt that has the name of your business prominently displayed? Or in taking your business cards everywhere you go and clipping your card to the slip when you pay for a purchase by card or cheque? Get in the habit of doing business promotion wherever you go and you'll be surprised how word-of-mouth builds.

If your leisure activity involves a group, you might ask if you can include your business information on all of their out-going paper, or ask if you can at least give everyone a brochure. And with any kind of group activity, there's always the opportunity to promote your business by letting other people know what you do and how it could benefit them. This doesn't mean that you talk about nothing else, but there are bound to be chances to talk about your business that crop up during normal conversation.

These ten business promotion ideas are just some of the ways you can promote your small business without spending a small fortune. With a little experimentation and time, you'll find out which of these ideas work best for you—and best get the word out about your small business.

SUGGESTED READINGS

Baker, Kim and Baker, Sunny. (1992). *How to Promote, Publicize & Advertise Your Growing Business: Getting the Word Out Without Spending a Fortune.* Wiley. New York.

Belch, George E. and Belch, Michael A. (1995). *Introduction to Advertising and Promotion: An Integrated Marketing Communications Perspective,* Chicago: Irwin.

Blake, G. and Bly, R.W. (1983). *How to Promote Your Own Business.* Plume Books. New York.

Dennison, Dell and Linda Toby. (1991). *The Advertising Handbook.*

Engel, James F., Warshaw, Martin R., Kinnear and Thomas C. (1994). *Promotional Strategy. Managing the Marketing Communications Process.* Burr Ridge, IL: Irwin.

Foster, Dennis L. (1988). *The Complete Franchise Book.* Prima Publishing and Communications.

Graydon, Shari (2003) *Made You Look - How Advertising Works and Why You Should Know.* Toronto: Annick Press.

Ind, Nicholas. (1993). *Great Advertising Campaigns. Goals and Accomplishments.* Lincolnwood, IL: NTC Publishing.

Kaatz, Ron. (1993). *Advertising and Marketing Checklists.* NTC Business Books.

Kendall, Robert (1992). *Public Relations Campaign Strategies.* New York: Harper Collins.

Kim Baker and Sunny Baker. (1992). *How to Promote, Publicize, and Advertise Your Growing Business: Getting the Word Out without Spending a Fortune.* John Wiley & Sons.

McElreath, Mark P. (1993). *Managing Systematic and Ethical Public Relations.* Madison, WI: Brown & Benchmark.

Murphy, John H. (1993). *Advertising and Marketing Communication Management.* Fort Worth, TX: Dryden.

Nager, Norman R. and Allen, T. Harrell (1995). *Public Relations Management by Objectives,* New York: Longman.

Schultz, Don and Barnes, Beth. (1995). *Strategic Advertising Campaigns,* Lincolnwood, IL: NTC Publishing.

_____________, Tannenbaum, Stanley I. (1988). *Essentials of Advertising Strategy.* Lincolnwood, IL: NTC Publishing.

_____________, Robinson, William A. (1982). *Sales Promotion Management.* Chicago: Crain Books.

Simmons, Robert E. (1990). *Communication Campaign Management: A systems approach.* New York: Longman.

Sissors, Jack Z. and Bumba, Lincoln. (1993). *Advertising media planning,* Lincolnwood IL: NTC Publishing.

Taylor, James W. (1993). *How to Develop a Successful Advertising Plan,* 2nd ed. Lincolnwood, IL: NTC Publishing.

Wernick, Andrew (1991). *Promotional Culture: Advertising, Ideology and Symbolic Expression.* London: Sage Publications Ltd.